P9-CBD-601

THE CRYPTOGRAM CHALLENGE

The Cryptogram Challenge

Published in the United States by Thunder's Mouth Press
245 West 17th Street, 11th Floor
New York, NY 10011

AVALON
publishing group incorporated

Copyright © Carlton Books Limited 2005

All rights reserved. No part of this publication may be reproduced,
stored in a retrieval system, or transmitted in any form or by any
means, electronic, mechanical, photocopying, recording or otherwise,
without the prior permission of the publisher, except for reviewers
wanting to excerpt material for review purposes.

Library of Congress Cataloging-in-Publication Data is available.

ISBN 1-56025-714-8

10 9 8 7 6 5 4 3 2 1

Project Editor: Martin Corteel
Project art direction: Clare Baggaley
Designer: Tanya Devonshire Jones
Production: Lisa French

Printed in Dubai
Distributed by
Publishers Group West
1700 Fourth Street
Berkeley, CA 94710

THE CRYPTOGRAM CHALLENGE

Over **150** Codes to Crack and **Ciphers** to Break

Robert Allen

THUNDER'S
MOUTH
PRESS

CONTENTS

CODE KEYS

Codes fall into two main types: secret key or public key. In a secret key code only the originator of the code knows how it works. However, if he wants to communicate with others he must share the secret otherwise they can't participate. This means he has constantly to make tough decisions about who he can trust. Eventually he can be pretty sure that someone will betray him. A public key code is much more ingenious. You allow anyone access to the method of encryption so that people can send you secret messages whenever they need to. However, only the owner of the code knows how to transform the coded messages back into plain language. This is clearly a much more secure method of coding but it has the disadvantage that you soon get into some complex maths and, whereas anyone can create or try to crack secret key codes, the higher echelons of cryptography are realistically only accessible only to mathematicians with access to a supercomputer.

The codes in this book are all 'simple' ones; in other words each symbol used will normally correspond to one letter of the alphabet (you will find just one exception to this rule). Do not, however, be fooled into thinking that the puzzles are easy. Some of them will yield their secrets readily but many others will cause you hours of thought. The really useful thing about codes is that even the simplest problem is often hard to crack unless you happen to think along the right lines.

SMNV - TNGN - RRTS - SWRT - RCTN
SHHT - HGRH - TLLD - NSMT
SRHC - RFBT - HGNH - TSWT

Look at this series of letters (above). Does it look difficult? In fact the puzzle is simple enough for a young child to solve given a quick flash of insight. The message is written backwards with vowels omitted and the consonants arbitrarily broken into groups of four. Now go back and take another look.
You'll solve the whole thing in seconds.

The object of this book is for you to have fun. All the codes used are solvable with a bit of logic and a lot of persistence. It would be easy enough to set problems that cannot be solved by an amateur but the resulting book wouldn't be much fun. Once you get the hang of the simple codes used here you should find that you can break them all… in time.

SUBSTITUTION CODES

Julius Caesar normally gets the credit for inventing the substitution code. It is still widely used and though in theory it is easy to crack you will find that it takes time and effort to do so. At its simplest the code works like this. You write the whole alphabet in a circle and then you write it again in a smaller circle. Start by putting the small circle within the larger one so that A = A, B = B, etc. Next you turn the inner circle so that, for example, A = C, B = D, etc. Now you have a code. Below you will find a diagram that shows you how to make a code wheel of your own. However, this does not mean that you can now solve every puzzle in the book. It is possible, as you will discover, to introduce many complications into what started as a simple code. When working with codes you must get used to the idea that letters can be used in place of numbers and vice versa. There is a table on page 9 to help you make the conversions quickly.

Remember that context is often a very good clue to code-breaking. If, for example, you manage to get the word 'beach' it should prompt you to look for associated words such as sea, sand, water, holiday and sunshine. Of course there is no guarantee that these words will occur but it is worth looking for them first before you try seeking more arcane solutions.

Finally, in case you think that all the old codes have long since been broken, here is an example of one that kept people guessing for 250 years and has only just been cracked. The so-called Shepherd's Monument at the Shugborough estate in Staffordshire, England bears a strange inscription (see below).

It defied all attempts to decode it and baffled some of the smartest brains in the business. It was said that the message was a clue to the location of the Holy Grail. Recently, however, an anonymous American came up with what appears to be the answer. According to him the inscription reads: Jesus (As Deity) Defy and it was put there by an eighteenth-century sect called the Priory of Sion. You may have read about them somewhere…

O.U.O. S.V.A.V.V

D   M

CODE-BREAKING TOOLS

26	A	1
25	B	2
24	C	3
23	D	4
22	E	5
21	F	6
20	G	7
19	H	8
18	I	9
17	J	10
16	K	11
15	L	12
14	M	13
13	N	14
12	O	15
11	P	16
10	Q	17
9	R	18
8	S	19
7	T	20
6	U	21
5	V	22
4	W	23
3	X	24
2	Y	25
1	Z	26

HERE ARE SOME ESSENTIAL TOOLS THAT ANY SELF-RESPECTING CODE BREAKER SHOULD NOT BE WITHOUT.

First, the alphanumeric values of the alphabet both forwards and backwards (left).

Remember that code writers often treat the alphabet as though it was written in a circle. So if you are counting letters and get to Z and run out, don't assume you have made a mistake but just keep counting. Here's a diagram to help:

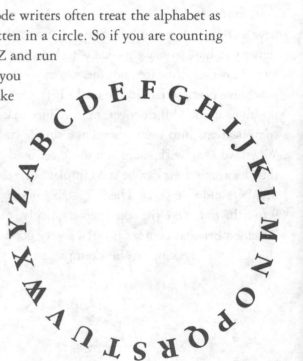

You will also need to make a code wheel. This makes the task of working with substitution codes much easier. You'll need to make two circles as shown below (the easiest way is to copy ours and cut them out) and fix them together by putting a split pin through the centre.

TOP WHEEL

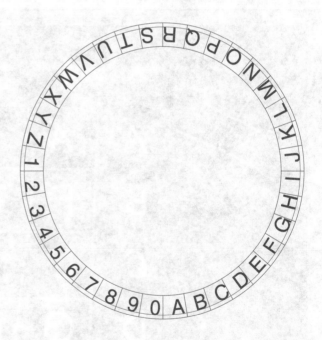

BOTTOM WHEEL

Finally, it is very useful to know the frequency with which letters occur in the English language. This will often give you your first vital clue as to how a code works. Here they are in order of frequency, starting from the left:

E T A O I N S H R D L U

Easy Peasy

We'll start with a few simple cryptograms to get you in the mood. The last one to make it through the Easy Peasy puzzles is a rotten egg! The simplest form of grid code involves a square divided into smaller squares to give a 5 x 5 block. You then write the letters of the alphabet from left to right starting at the left of the top row and working down to the bottom right. I and J are treated as the same letter. You then write the letters A to E down the left hand side of the block and the numbers 1 to 5 along the top. It will look like this:

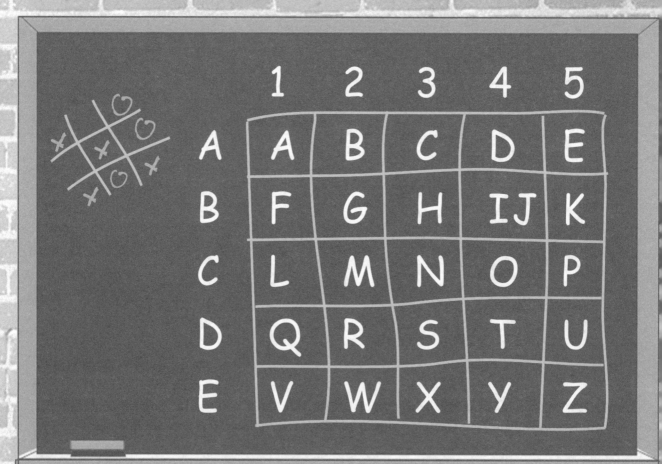

	1	2	3	4	5
A	A	B	C	D	E
B	F	G	H	IJ	K
C	L	M	N	O	P
D	Q	R	S	T	U
E	V	W	X	Y	Z

Now you can refer to any letter within the block by giving its coordinates, so A1 will stand for A and E5 will be Z. Though the basic idea is simple enough there is any number of ways in which the grid can be formed. The message below was constructed using the grid system. Can you work out what shape grid we used and then decode the message?

G3	F1	H3	E3
C3	H1	C3	E2
C2	G3	B2	H3
F1	E2	E3	C3
C2	F2	H1	E2
F1	B2	E2	H3
B2	A3	G2	
A3	B3	D3	

Answer on Page 180

Easy peasy

The cipher on the right is pretty straightforward. In fact, if you have your computer handy, you could crack the code in next to no time, especially if you recognize the symbols I have used. Even if the symbols don't immediately mean anything to you they should not be too hard to crack — it will just take a bit of trial and error. Work first on the snowflake and then have a guess at the flag. Once you have those the rest will follow quickly. The sentence is a very well-known one which you will quickly recognize.

Answer on Page 180

MORSE MUDDLE

 ere is a chance to have fun with Morse code. A complication has been introduced so that, even when you are on the right track, you may not see which way to go next.

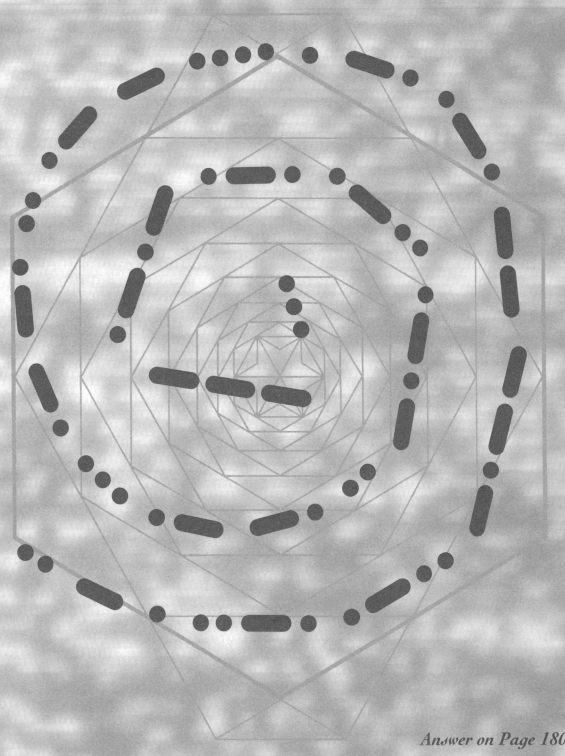

Answer on Page 180

The text below is very famous. The author was blind which should narrow your search a bit. Naturally before we introduced this rather fancy font we did something tricky to the text but, if you have an inkling about the author, you shouldn't find the code too hard to break.

DA
RK

ST
OR
Y

DARK STORY

Answer on Page 180

A Good-Humoured Message

Six words related to good humour are hidden below. Discover what they have in common and you will be able to find all six.

ALABASTER
ABASEMENT
SCUTTLE
GRUDGE
BEHEAD

AMERICA
BIBULOUS
CRACKERJACK
WIDTH
REHOUSE

AMITY
ABETTER
ACROSTIC
DRIBBLE
EYES

YAHOO
BATTLE
ECPHONESIS
BEDPOST
OBEY

BAFFLE
ABUNDANCE
PICNIC
KIDNAP
HOCKEY

PASSED
BUTLER
ACNE
KIDNEYS
ABBEY

Answer on Page 180

6 OF THE BEST:

Biblical characters

The grid below contains six biblical characters carefully concealed. They are not necessarily the most famous people in the Bible but they all come from the Old Testament and, even if you have only the slightest acquaintance with scripture, you will know the names. They have been encoded in several different ways.

```
J B A B U Z V E N P
I N O U P K Z R I D
F I D C A D C T V O
S G Q O V L E S I D
N V W W B D L E Q F
J N P G A V I U M K
Q F B N C L D A E L
N M A Z W O O P L R
S I D I O M I P T V
M H Y E D A R G I K
```

A little alchemy

The text below is written in a mysterious alchemical language that can only be understood by fully qualified wizards, warlocks and other magical folk. No, only kidding. It is actually English that has been disguised with a fancy font. You should, with a bit of effort, be able to reveal the plain text.

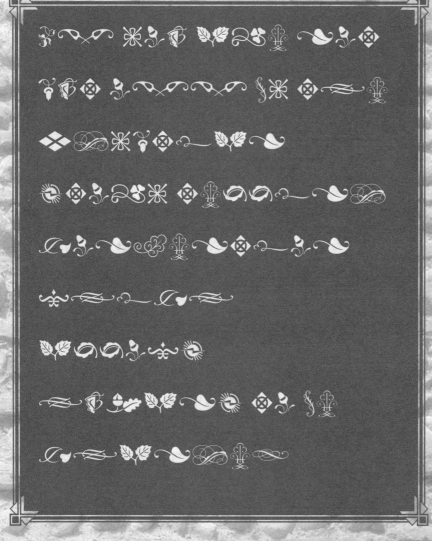

A little alchemy

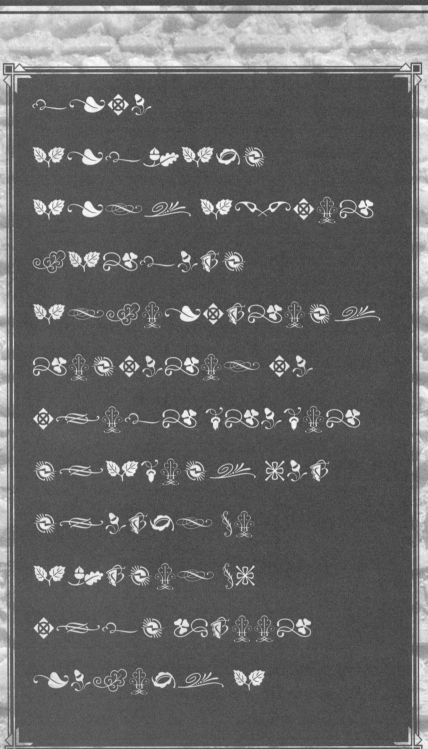

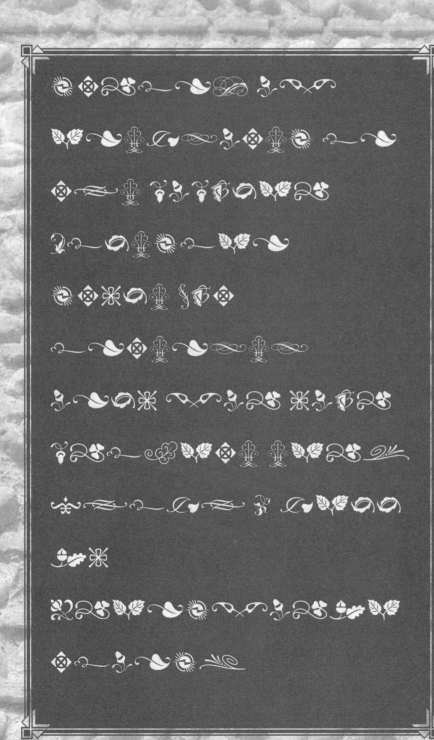

A little alchemy

Answer on Page 180

A write muddle

Below you will see four books each by a famous author. The authors' names are, of course, coded and your challenge is to work out who wrote each one. To give you a clue just one word from the title of each book is given uncoded.

GUIDE

SMDSLGD

KILL

LRPRH

Jones

GNDLFYRNH

WIND

LLHCTMTRGRM

Bright Ideas

These puzzles are called Bright Ideas because in them there lurk the names of people famous for their clever notions. The people come from all over the world and may be living or dead. There is no single way to tackle these puzzles as each is constructed on a different principle. Let's see how you get on.

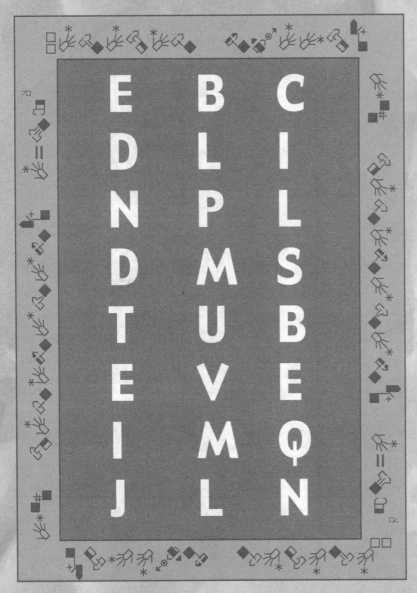

E B C
D L I
N P L
D M S
T U B
E V E
I M Q
J L N

Answers on Page 180 & 181

A Place of One's Own

B elow you will find six words to do with living accommodation hidden among the verbiage. Can you find them all?

BADGE
FROWNING
DEFEND
MAESTRO
FINAL

AMENDS
TALENT
BATON
BEIGE
TORRENT

BELIEVE
COMPASS
ZULU
OREGANO
ATTACH

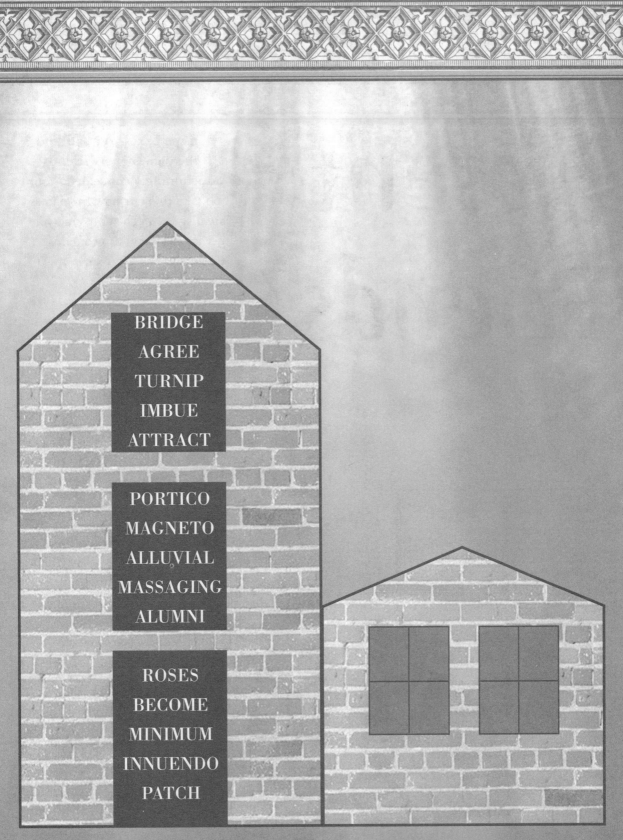

BRIDGE
AGREE
TURNIP
IMBUE
ATTRACT

PORTICO
MAGNETO
ALLUVIAL
MASSAGING
ALUMNI

ROSES
BECOME
MINIMUM
INNUENDO
PATCH

Answer on Page 181

Absent Friends?

In the boxes you will find the names of six friends cunningly concealed. Your job is to find out how the names are disguised. The only clue you get is that the group contains three boys and three girls.

D	V
M	Y

A	R
A	E

D	A
J	K

C	E
N	I

S	N
K	T

E	A
A	E

Answer on Page 181

Blind Logic

Braille, as everybody knows, is a system that allows blind people to read by touch. To us it may look clumsy, but if you are fully trained in it you can read at about the same speed as a sighted person. The following message is just straightforward Braille. If you wanted to you could go to a website, download the whole alphabet and work out what I had written in a matter of a couple of minutes. But what fun would that be?

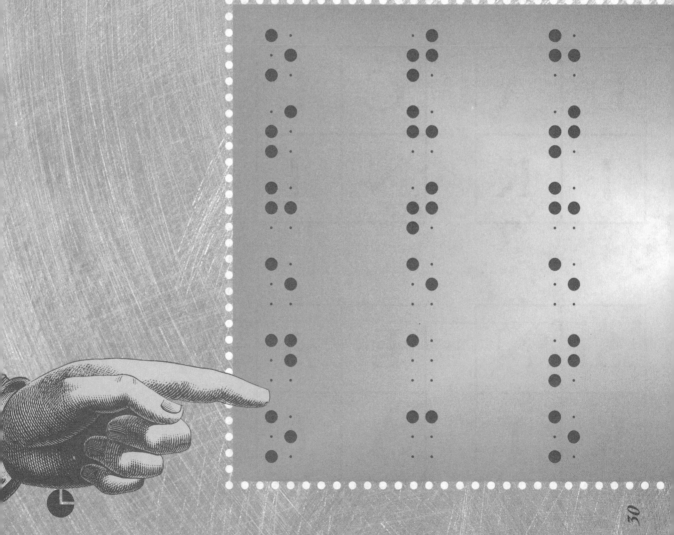

Try to work it out without looking it up. There is a certain logic to the letters, and once you have discovered it you will find that translating becomes easier.

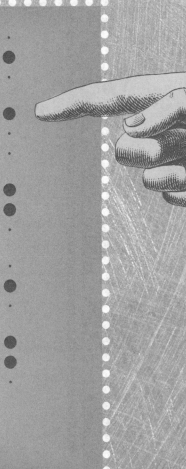

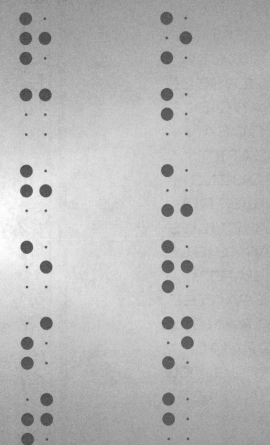

31

Answer on Page 181

Artfully Concealed

Below you will find the names of three artists hidden. One of them is Turner and if you can find him you can probably find the others as well.

THIMBLE
ETERNAL
NINETY
OVERSEER
MANDIBLE
OCEAN
SAFETY
SQUELCH
AUSTRIA
CALCULUS
INVINCIBLE
PARTY
REPARTEE
ESTRANGED
NORMALITY
REFORMED
UNTRIED
TRAMPOLINE

T he words below conceal six words with a religious flavour.

AMEN CORNER

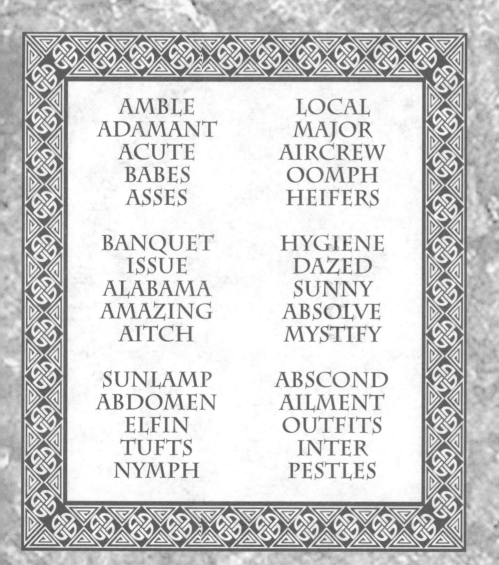

AMBLE	LOCAL
ADAMANT	MAJOR
ACUTE	AIRCREW
BABES	OOMPH
ASSES	HEIFERS
BANQUET	HYGIENE
ISSUE	DAZED
ALABAMA	SUNNY
AMAZING	ABSOLVE
AITCH	MYSTIFY
SUNLAMP	ABSCOND
ABDOMEN	AILMENT
ELFIN	OUTFITS
TUFTS	INTER
NYMPH	PESTLES

Answer on Page 181

Circular Conundrum

T he numbers below have a book title among them. Can you find it?

13-2-8-15-17-19-3-21-9-11-10-22-9-25-7-14-3-4-7-2-15-19-9-20-1-18-24-6-4-20-7-9-15-3-24-11-20-12-9-18-5-13-12-3-13-4-7-1-6-23

The acrostic below conceals the name of a lady known for her adventurous spirit. She's feisty, physically tough and prone to acts of violence but, for those with the knack, she's easy to control. Who is she?

HIDDEN
HIDDEN

ADVENTURER
ADVENTURER

```
        B
        U
B U F F Y        K
        A        I
        L        N
        O        G
W I L L I A M T E L L
        B        A
        A S T E R I X                              H
        I        T                        R O B R O Y
        L        H                                A
        L        U R O B E R T B R U C E           R
                                    C              R
                        D A N I E L B O O N E      Y
                        R                          P
                        A                          O
                        Z                          T
                        Y                          T
            D A V Y C R O C K E T T                E
                        O                          R
                        R
                        S
                        E
        I N D I A N A J O N E S
```

Answers on Page 181

Blind Logic

N ow you are getting to grips with the Braille alphabet here is another variation for you to try. How much do I want to tell you about this? Hmmm, not much at all really. It's far more fun to let you work it out. Let's just say that working out the letters that the Braille signs stand for won't do you much good. However, if you really don't catch on to what I'm doing a bit of research on one of the many Braille internet sites will help. One more thing: a blind person would probably get my drift quite quickly but would complain that a vital piece of information had been missed out.

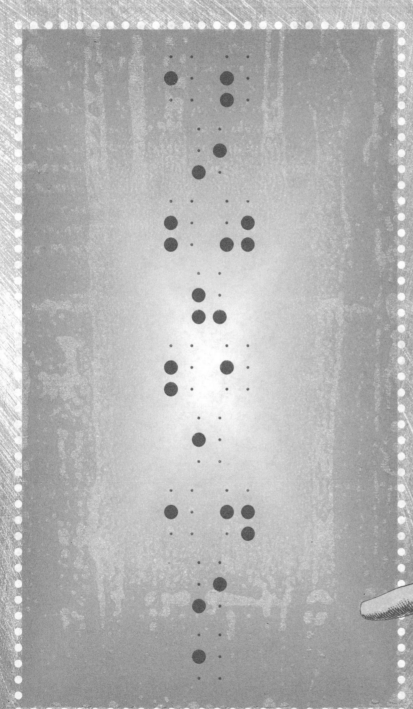

Answer on Page 181

Bright Ideas

Here's another famous name cunningly concealed. Be careful not to let yourself be fooled into ignoring the obvious. Misleading puzzle-solvers by making them search for hidden subleties that don't exist is an old trick. This one is much easier than it looks at first sight.

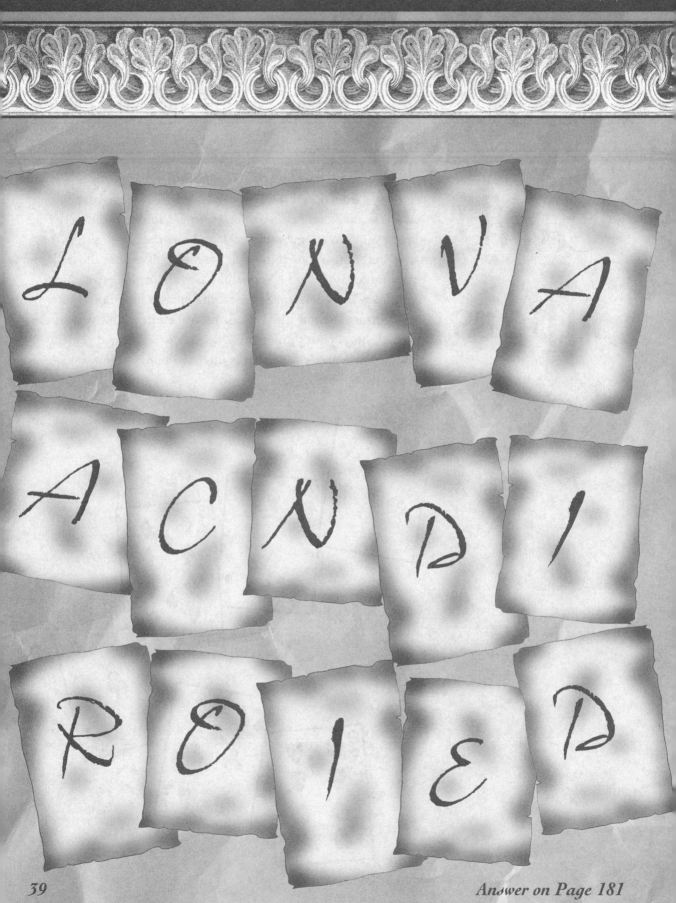

Answer on Page 181

Card Capers

As you can see, the code below is based on a traditional pack of cards. I discovered to my joy that cards are just ideal for making a simple but effective code. Why? Well, get out a pack and sort them into suits. You may well notice something that makes a bell ring at the back of your mind. But there is something else about this puzzle that will keep you guessing. So far all the puzzles have been quite straightforward and I have made no real effort to put you off the scent. This time it's different. This code is basically dishonest and contains an element that is intended purely to make life hard for you.

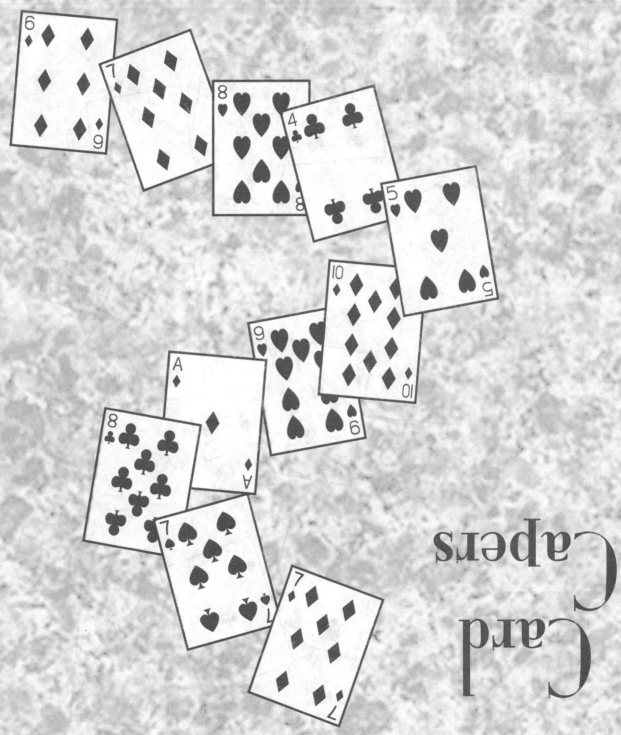

Card Capers

Card
Capers

Card Capers

Answer on Page 181

HIDDEN HEROINES

The grid contains the names of two young actresses. One of them has a medical connection and the other has been in a film set at sea. They have also appeared in a film together.

N	K	A	A	R	E	M
I	G	H	R	Y	A	L
D	N	G	T	P	A	N
I	I	R	R	E	K

Answer on Page 182

CHINESE CHALLENGE 1

You don't read Chinese? Never mind, because to solve this puzzle you don't have to. In fact, if you were to take it down to the local Chinese takeaway and show it to the friendly proprietor he would confess himself completely confused. The characters used are all genuine

豆 八八 黑 斗

面 黑 八八 土

烏 林 一 二

Chinese, but being able to read them would just muddle you. Try to think what else they could mean. Being able to count would be a real help (and, yes, that is a BIG clue).

斗　豆豆　非　　生

豆豆　非　生生　生

生　八　生　一　生生

林

Answer on Page 182

CHINESE CHALLENGE 1

Cash Crisis

3-1-19-8 3-18-9-19-9-19 3-1-19-8 3-18-9-19-9-19 3-1-19-8 3-18-9-19-9-19 3-1-19-8 3-18-9-19-9-19 3-1-19-8 3-18-9-19-9-19

Below you will find six words that have been cunningly concealed. They all have a financial connection.

PUMP
RATIONAL
QUAKER
HANNIBAL
BUDGET

GARAGE
REALIZE
XERXES
JUICE
KILO

ENTIRE
XENOPHOBIC
FOREIGNER
NATIVE
VALUATION

FORDE
HANDLE
QUAVER
WISCONSIN
VIVID

VENUE
SAFFRON
HANDLE
QUELL
GARNISH

GARBAGE
LUCKY
PARAMEDIC
HARSHLY
VENUSIAN

Answer on Page 182

CD DILEMMA

Here you wil find six CD's each from a different band. On each CD is one word from one of the band's well known songs. That is the only clue you'll get. The name of each band appears in code below. Your task is to work out all six names.

BICYCLE

34-42-10-10-28

CLOUD

36-30-24-24-18-28-14-
38-40-30-28-10-38

MISERY

14-36-10-10-28-8-2-50

FALL

36-2-52-30-36-24-
18-14-16-40

FIELDS

4-10-2-40-24-10-38

BROTHERS

8-18-36-10-38-40-
36-2-18-40-38

Answer on Page 182

Concealed Composers

B elow you will find the names of three classical composers disguised. One of them is Mozart. If you can find him, you should be able to find the others as well.

ENSEMBLE

ORB

INVENT

BATH

ALLIANCE

FALLEN

LIBIDO

ROMANOV

INVOICE

MAGENTA

FAMILIAR

APART

TOPAZ

FARM

KANGAROO

CONDEMN

HIPPOPOTAMI

KIND

NUMBER

ALBINO

TOO

KEBAB

Answer on Page 182

CONCEALED CROOK

One of the bad guys from America's past is concealed among a random assortment of respectable people in the grid below. He is going by his nickname to avoid recognition. Can you find him?

You ain't seen nuthin'

SINATRA

GENE PITNEY

GOLDFINGER

JODIE FOSTER

FREDDIEMERCURY

SHARONOSBOURNE

BARBIE

BRADPITT

DONALDDUCK

Answer on Page 182

Crossword

T he crossword here contains the names of a number of countries. All you have to do is decode them.

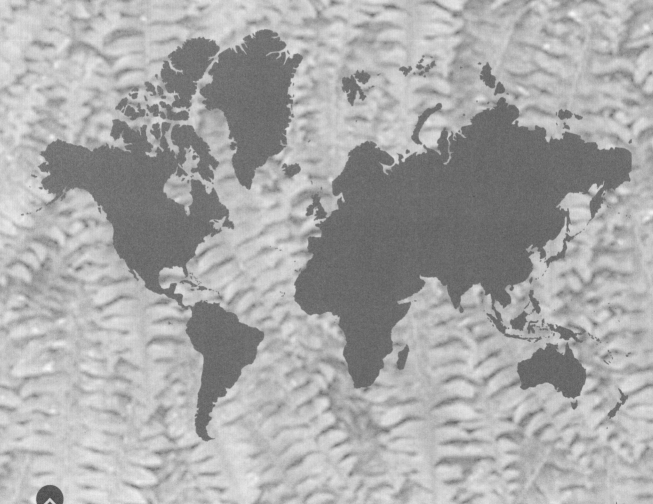

Answer on Page 182

Card Capers

Assuming you have solved the first of the card capers, you will now be full of confidence that you can solve the second. Hah! That's what you think! But I know different. What follows is a tricky variation on the first puzzle. Let's see how you cope when playing with someone who cheats at cards.

Card
Capers

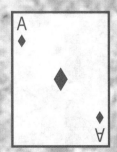

Answer on Page 182

Crypto Wordsearch

Here we have a variation on the ever-popular wordsearch. Below you will find a grid in which we have concealed the names of a dozen film stars. There is one tiny problem. The letters of their names have been displaced one place in the alphabet. some have been moved one place forwards and some one place backwards. See how many you can find. The names to look for are:

Julia Roberts

Robert Redford

Colin Firth

Hugh Grant

Ashley Olsen

Brad Pitt

Angelina Jolie

Cameron Diaz

Halle Berry

Liam Neeson

Donald Sutherland

Pierce Brosnan

```
B G H T E O P S D E J U P L M N W T S F
C F R T H G X W Y U O I P L K J N F T M
V T R S Q B G T N H Y O P I L K J M N Y
C T Y H G E U Y I O P R N M B T R E S T
V G T I U Y B B M H S W R E T D G T D W
S G T Y H A S E T O B K N S E R T Y N M
V Q R T Y B F W C F G N Y T A S D E F J
C N E F T Q J F S D F C S P T M B M B B
E A C F R G T Y U J M F P O W G T H D N
C D C V R T S H G W U Y F T E T H O O M
X Q S S Z E M O W Q W D E G T Y H Y U O F
D S B A D K V M B J S P C F S U T V Y F
B Q E V Y T M O P L K Q T E U T U I O T
N D Q B T Y U P X E D R T O P B Q W G P
F C J B A S E R T G Y T Y U I T T N T O M
S E U Y A X C T W U T R B O N I W V F M
P N U T V R T N A S W N Y P R M V T I O
O Q C E V T R T Y U I M Y W E F E S H T
E C S D M I O G J S U I C R Z E V S C
J Z I O C E B T Y H B Y I O P P W V B N
B W D E R G Y T O I D F E B T M N Y O B
A C E T R Q P O I B G T Y O I T R E U B
C E R I B M M F C F S S Z B T P B T Y P
V R G T F H N B N Y D E T T R O V R E N
T F T T W Y R G R O P T E W N H W T R T
R Y T Y D N E B O E F M J O B K P M J F
E R G P T O G V R T Y E O P B T B T P V
G E P M B M E T V U I F S M B M E X W T
T W W V V P H Q D R T Y N H Y E D R F T
N E R B T I M F Z P M T R O C Y E O U P
```

Answer on Page 183

I f you look carefully you will discover a number of hidden words all connected with music.

Dance Dilemma

ELDER
MACHINE
ANNEX
OCCULT
PERPETUITY

FILM
MUNICIPAL
INSTITUTION
POISONOUS
CUPCAKE

PULP
MOMENT
INLAND
OKLAHOMA
PARTITION

RAILWAY
EMANCIPATION
UNLUCKY
OTHERWISE
LEIPZIG

WALRUS
MUTUAL
ENMESH
OBESITY
PALSY

CARDINALS
SMASHING
UNLOVELY
OSTRACISM
APACHE

Dance Dilemma

Answer on Page 183

DEAF

◆〰♏□◆♒♏&
♌□♋□◆■♐⚹□⊠♂◆

WORDS

○□♋◆♏♏□◆〰
♏●♋♋⌘♒⊠♎♋♐

You will no doubt have noticed that deaf people have a sign language that allows them to communicate by means of hand gestures. This is not strictly speaking a code because the meaning of the gestures is well known among those who need to use them. They do, however, have the unintended effect of keeping most people in ignorance about what they see being discussed. Some words, names for example, cannot be expressed in single gestures but have to be spelt out using a special finger-spelling system. Each of the letters of the alphabet has its own gesture. Now this is particularly useful should you wish to devise ciphers to convey secret messages. The text on this page is composed purely of the standard finger-spelling system. If you wanted to cheat, you could simply look up this system and you could, after a little practice, read the message opposite. However, that would spoil the fun, wouldn't it? The idea is to puzzle the meaning out for yourself. Once you have done that you can go on to work on other puzzles that look similar but, for one reason or another, are harder to crack. Make sure you decode this page first because, if you don't, you will find decoding the others much more difficult.

Answer on Page 183

CHINESE CHALLENGE

"What more Chinese?" I hear you cry. "Enough already!" Try just one more and then we'll think up a new torture, erm I mean puzzle. This one is related to the first one you tried but I have introduced a cunning twist that will take some time to unravel. As with all good twists it is really very simple but even so, it might give you a problem or two before you solve it.

大一　大一　爪四　爪一　坐

爪四　杧三　爪三　爪四　杧三

旭四　枯五　未爪　十　大三

卜　杧三　禾一

Answer on Page 183

Deaf

Words

I f you have solved the first puzzle using the finger-spelling alphabet for the deaf then you are in a good position to try this one. The first thing you will notice is that if you use the solution to the last puzzle as a basis for solving this one all you get as a reward for your efforts is gibberish. Don't be disheartened! You are on the right track but a new twist has been added in order to make things more interesting. It's surprising just how difficult a cipher can be even if you add only minor variations to it. You hear a lot about there being no such thing as an unbreakable code and that well may be true. But with a little cunning you can certainly make the code breaker sweat a bit.

One more thing: the last puzzle was easy to solve because once you started to make a little progress you found that you recognized the sentence I had encoded. The one opposite is a perfectly good sentence but its meaning won't convey anything to you.

71

Answer on Page 183

Honourable Speech

The grid below contains part of a well-known speech. Of course, you son't need me to tell you that the numbers are alphanumeric values, but you might find they don't give you exactly the answer you expect. Also, it might take you a while to work out how the speech has been inserted in the grid.

16	15	2	21	18	25	3	1
5	13	5	14	12	5	14	5
13	25	17	18	15	13	4	17
15	18	4	10	18	1	13	1
13	3	16	14	5	7	14	5	18
7	7	14	21	15	3	17	25	14
8	17	18	1	5	18	21	15	15
5	17	7	1	18	20	15	16	16

House Hunting

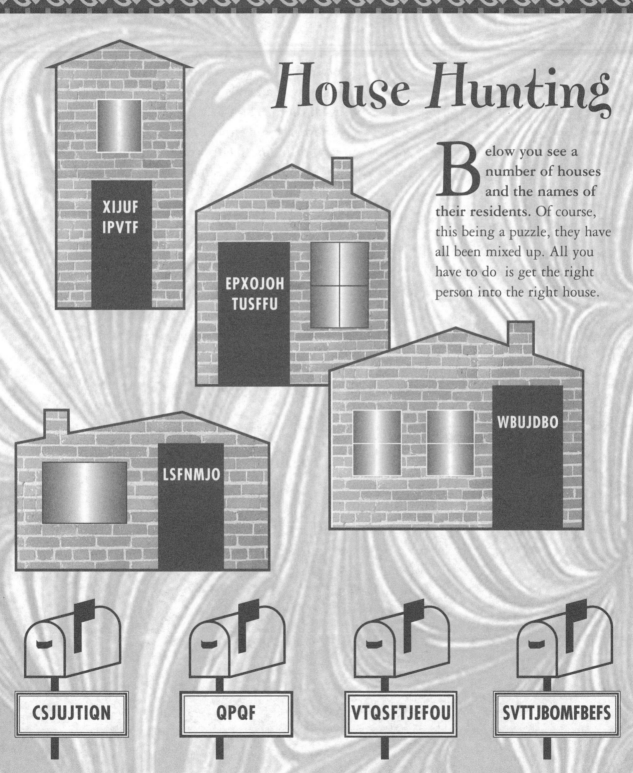

Below you see a number of houses and the names of their residents. Of course, this being a puzzle, they have all been mixed up. All you have to do is get the right person into the right house.

XIJUF IPVTF

EPXOJOH TUSFFU

WBUJDBO

LSFNMJO

CSJUJTIQN

QPQF

VTQSFTJEFOU

SVTTJBOMFBEFS

73

Answers on Pages 183 & 184

Blind Logic

Now that you have some familiarity with Braille signs we can start to do more complicated things with them. There may be some in this puzzle that you do not know. You can either be brave and try to work it out or you can look them up. In either case, you will not find this puzzle as easy to crack as the last one.

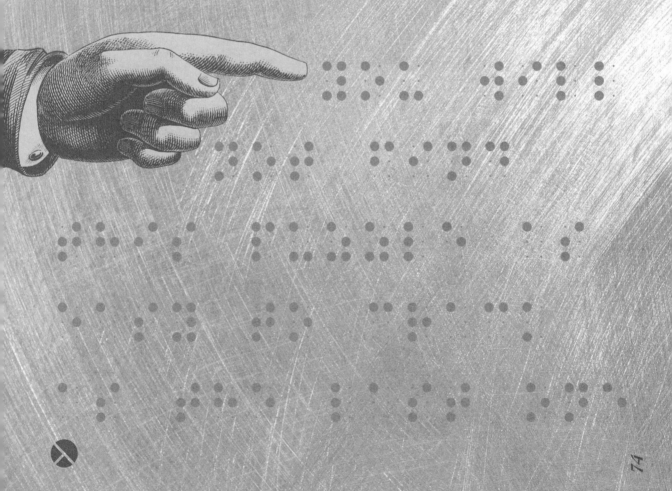

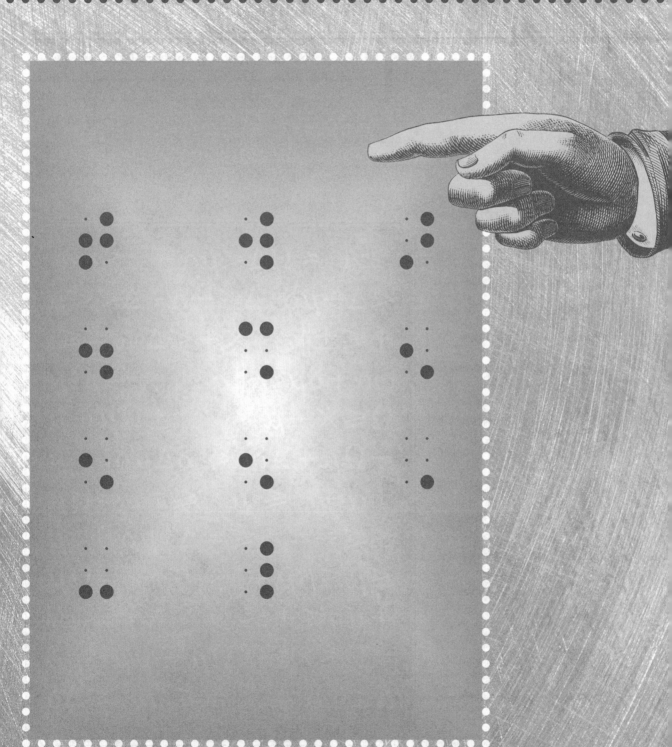

Answer on Page 184

LONG JOURNEY

There is absolutely nothing mysterious about the text that follows. It is the beginning of a well-known novel chosen mainly because it is long out of copyright. The strange letters are in an unusual font. All you have to do now is try to turn it into English.

$$\geq + \quad \approx \Omega \Delta < \mu \alpha - \quad ^- \leqslant \omega \omega$$
$$< \Delta \div \mu \delta \quad \Delta \circ \quad - \alpha \div \Delta << \mu$$
$$+ \leqslant \pm \| \quad ^- \times + < \Delta \circ \omega = \leqslant \circ$$
$$\omega \alpha + \delta \mu \circ - \| \qquad = \Omega \mu$$
$$\Omega \leqslant \times - \mu \qquad \pm \Omega \mu + \mu$$
$$- \Omega \mu + \Delta \delta \alpha \circ \quad \delta \Delta \mu \delta | \quad \} \mu$$
$$\pm \alpha - \quad \leqslant \circ \mu \quad \leqslant \pi \quad = \Omega \mu$$
$$\leqslant \leqslant - = \quad \circ \leqslant = \Delta \gamma \mu \alpha \beta < \mu$$
$$\leqslant \mu \leqslant \beta \mu + - \quad \leqslant \pi \quad = \Omega \mu$$
$$+ \mu \pi \leqslant + \leqslant \qquad \sqrt{} < \times \beta \|$$
$$= \Omega \leqslant \times \omega \Omega \quad \Omega \mu - \mu \mu \leqslant \mu \delta$$
$$\alpha < \pm \alpha \infty - \quad = \leqslant \quad \alpha \div \leqslant \Delta \delta$$

$\alpha = \ = \ + \ \alpha \ \gamma \ = \ \Delta \ \circ \ \omega$

$\alpha = = \mu \circ = \Delta \leqslant \circ ' \quad \Delta \circ \quad \alpha \circ$

$\mu \circ \Delta \omega \leq \alpha = \Delta \gamma \alpha < \ \sim \mu + \circ$

$- \leqslant \circ \alpha \omega \mu \| \qquad \alpha \beta \leqslant \times =$

$\pm \Omega \leqslant \leq \ < \Delta = = < \mu \ \pm \alpha -$

$\Sigma \circ \leqslant \pm \circ \ \mu \varnothing \gamma \mu \sim = \ = \Omega \alpha =$

$\Omega \mu \quad \pm \alpha - \quad \alpha \quad \sim \leqslant < \circ$

$\Delta - \Omega \mu \delta \ \leq \alpha \circ \ \leq \pi \ = \Omega \mu$

$\pm \leqslant + < \delta | \qquad \approx \mu \leqslant \sim < \mu$

$- \alpha \Delta \delta \quad = \Omega \alpha = \qquad \Omega \mu$

$+ \mu - \mu \leq \beta < \mu \delta \ ^- \infty + \leqslant \circ$

$\alpha = \quad < \mu \alpha - = \quad = \Omega \alpha =$

LONG JOURNEY

$$\Omega\Delta- \qquad \Omega\mu\alpha\delta \qquad \pm\alpha-$$
$$^-\infty+\leqslant\circ\Delta\gamma' \quad \beta\times= \quad \Omega\mu$$
$$\pm\alpha- \qquad \alpha \qquad \beta\mu\alpha+\delta\mu\delta\|$$
$$=+\alpha\circ\Omega\times\Delta< \quad ^-\infty+\leqslant\circ\|$$
$$\pm\Omega\leqslant \quad \leqslant\Delta\omega\Omega= \quad <\Delta\div\mu$$
$$\leqslant\circ \qquad \alpha \qquad =\Omega\leqslant\times-\alpha\circ\delta$$
$$\infty\mu\alpha+- \qquad \pm\Delta=\Omega\leqslant\times=$$
$$\omega+\leqslant\pm\Delta\circ\omega \quad \leqslant<\delta|$$
$$\qquad \sqrt{}\mu+=\alpha\Delta\circ<\infty \qquad \alpha\circ$$
$$\sqrt{}\circ\omega<\Delta-\Omega\leq\alpha\circ\| \ \{ \ \pm\alpha-$$
$$\leq\leqslant+\mu \qquad \delta\leqslant\times\beta=\pi\times<$$
$$\pm\Omega\mu=\Omega\mu+ \ ^-\leqslant\omega \pm\alpha-$$
$$\alpha \ >\leqslant\circ\delta\leqslant\circ\mu+| \ \}\mu \ \pm\alpha-$$
$$\circ\mu\div\mu+ \qquad -\mu\mu\circ \qquad \leqslant\circ$$
$$\sqrt{}\Omega\alpha\circ\omega\mu\|\circ\leqslant= \ \alpha= \ =\Omega\mu$$
$$^-\alpha\circ\Sigma\| \ \circ\leqslant+ \ \ \Delta\circ \ \ =\Omega\mu$$

γ≤×∘=Δ∘ω +≤≤≤−
≤π =Ωμ √Δ=∞ ′ ∘≤
−ΩΔ∼− μ÷μ+ γα≤μ
Δ∘=≤ >≤∘δ≤∘ δ≤γΣ−
≤π ±ΩΔγΩ Ωμ ±α−
=Ωμ ≤±∘μ+′ Ωμ Ωαδ
∘≤   ∼×β<Δγ
μ≤∼<≤∞≤μ∘=′   Ωμ
Ωαδ   ∘μ÷μ+   βμμ∘
μ∘=μ+μδ α= α∘∞ ≤π
=Ωμ {∞− ≤π √≤×+=‖
≤+ {+α∞−   {∞‖ ∘≤+
Ωαδ   ΩΔ−   ÷≤Δγμ
μ÷μ+ +μ−≤×∘δμδ Δ∘
=Ωμ   √≤×+=   ≤π
√Ωα∘γμ+∞|

Answer on Page 184

Find the Lady

Concealed among this list of words is the name of a famous American lady. Her name is hidden but not encoded. you can see all the letters you need right now!

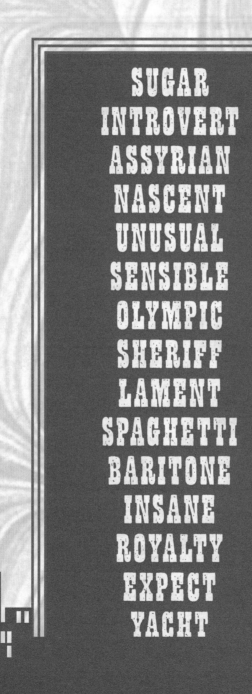

SUGAR
INTROVERT
ASSYRIAN
NASCENT
UNUSUAL
SENSIBLE
OLYMPIC
SHERIFF
LAMENT
SPAGHETTI
BARITONE
INSANE
ROYALTY
EXPECT
YACHT

Answer on Page 184

Crossword

The crossword below contains the names of a number of places in code. With a bit of persistence you should be able to turn them back into plain language.

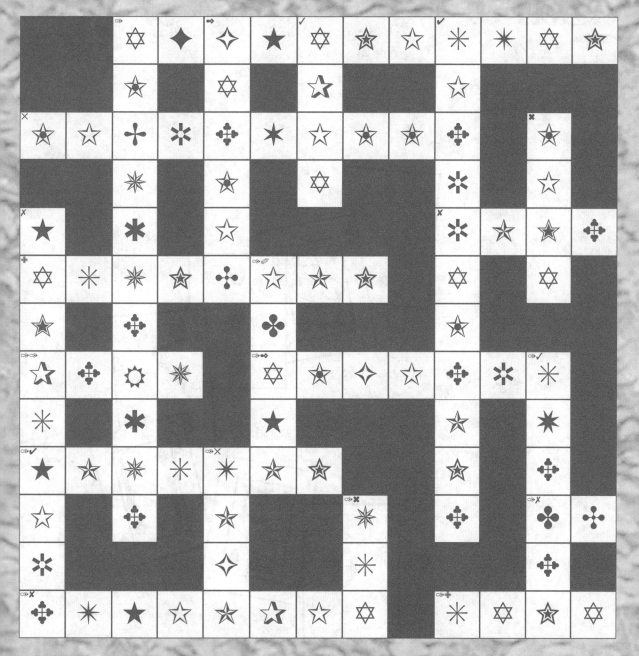

Answer on Page 184

Card Capers

Here we have another card trick for you to grapple with. This isn't going to be easy so take a deep breath before you start. The trouble is that, even if you start to work with the right method, your results will still look like gibberish until you spot the fiendish trick that has been played on you.

Card
Capers

Card
Capers

Card Capers

Answer on Page 184

Crossword

The crossword below contains the names of a number of US presidents. They have been coded in slightly differnt ways and therefore, where names cross, a letter is missing. Even so, you should be able to work them all out with a bit of persistence.

Answer on Page 185

SILLY SEMAPHORE

Semaphore was used to send messages over fairly short distances. It only works if you can see the man with the flags (so it's pretty useless at night). It was once much used by navies around the world but has long been eclipsed by much more efficient methods. Probably the only people who still bother with it are Boy Scouts so, if you get really stuck on this section, you'll have to search for a Scout to help you. Tell him it counts as his good deed for the day. The first puzzle is perfectly straighforward. I have used semaphore to spell out a short messge. See if you can work out what it is without cheating. As with Braille, semaphore does have a sort of logic that allows you to work out the letters. Finally, here's a clue: famous last words.

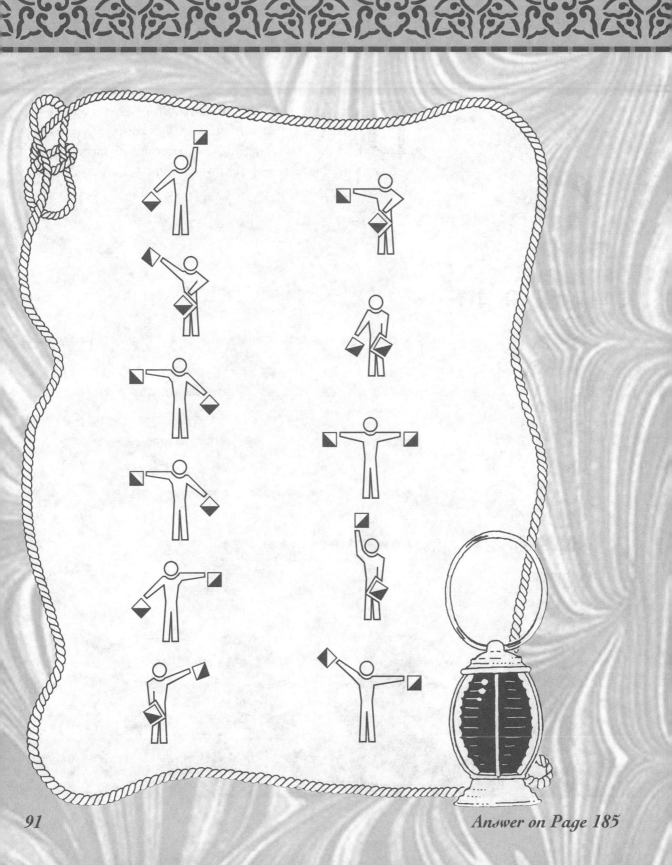

Answer on Page 185

Incognito

B elow you will find the name of one of our secret agents. If you answer the questions correctly you will find that, by taking the first letter of each answer, you will get a jumble of letters that, when properly decoded, reveal the identity of the spy.

Incognito

1. Ancient god with two faces

2. Lover's saint

3. US State

4. Proper name of "Sioux" tribe

5. Workers' organization

6. Used in sunny weather

7. Capital of Ecuador

8. Mafia code of silence

9. Prefix meaning "thousand"

10. Brown pigment

Answer on Page 185

Deaf

This puzzle may look just like the others involving the finger-spelling alphabet but, of course, it isn't. The difficulties are considerable. The puzzle involves a piece of apparatus that you almost cerainly own. It is up to you to work out what it is and how it has been used. Even when you have all this information you will find that the puzzle still does not make perfect sense. However, just to give you a little encouragement, the sentence you are asked to decode is one you will probably have heard before.

Words

Answer on Page 185

Easy Peasy

People make the mistake of assuming that codes have to be complicated whereas in fact even very simple devices can cause the solver problems. If you go looking for deviousness where it doesn't exist, you can often end up not seeing the thing that is right in front of your eyes. The cipher you see below is just about the simplest there is, even so, there will be some readers who don't catch on and will kick themselves when they finally look up the answer. See how long it takes you. Anything over a couple of minutes is a cause for shame.

```
S M E L B        E D E L P
O R P R E        M I S Y R
V L O S E        E V N E V
H T E S U        E T C A F
A C N A C        N I S A E
S E C I V        R E H W
```

xlwvh wl

mlg szev gl yv

xlnkorxzgvw

DETAC   IMUSS

ILPMO   AFOEK

CEBOT   ATSIM

EVAHS   EHTEK

EDOCT   AMELP

AHTGN   TR SP

Answer on Page 185

FOR A RAINY AFTER- NOON

Before you start on this puzzle be warned:it is VERY DIFFICULT INDEED. It may look just like previous cryptograms and you may think that all you have to do is guess some of the most frequent letters and then use common sense to fill in the gaps. That is not true. There is a really nasty complication included and you should only attempt the puzzle if you are willing to get very, very frustrated. This puzzle is ideal for one of those rainy days when you really can't do much else.

80ᒋᗰᗩᗰ ƎIYS Iᗰ SᖶƎᑎIƎᗰ OᖴᖇIS

ᗩᗷSOᒍYTI ᒍᑎOᗷATAᗰ ƎSSE YOᗰƎᑎ Iᗰ

TᗩIᗰIS ET ᒍOᗰSƎᑎSYS Iᗰ ƎO

ᗰᗑOᗩTAᒍIYᗰ OᗑᗷƎᗰ ATEᒍᒍAᑎTIYᗰ,

SEᑎ ET AᑎYᗰƎᑎTA ᑫᗩᗑᗰ ᑎOᒍƎᑎT,

AᑫYᒍIᗷ SIᒍAT ᑫYIA TAᒍIS 8IᒍYᑫA

OℲℲℲℲℲS SℲI ℲℲℲℲℲℲS ℲℲℲℲℲ IℲ SℲSℲ
ℲℲℲℲS ℲSℲ ℲℲℲℲℲℲℲℲℲ ℲSℲℲ ℲℲℲℲ ℲℲ
ℲℲℲℲℲℲℲ ℲℲℲℲℲℲℲ ℲℲ ℲℲℲℲℲℲℲℲℲℲ
ℲℲℲ ℲℲℲℲℲ ℲℲℲ ℲℲℲℲℲℲℲℲ ℲℲℲ ℲℲℲℲℲ ℲℲℲ
ℲℲℲℲℲℲℲ ℲℲℲℲℲ SℲI ℲℲℲℲℲℲℲS SℲℲℲℲℲℲS,
ℲℲℲ ℲℲℲℲ ℲℲℲ ℲℲℲℲℲℲ, ℲℲℲ SℲℲℲℲℲℲ
ℲℲℲℲI ℲℲℲ ℲℲℲℲℲℲℲℲℲ, ℲℲℲℲS
ℲℲℲℲℲℲℲ ℲSℲ ℲℲℲℲℲℲℲℲ Ⅎ
ℲℲℲℲℲℲℲ ℲℲℲℲℲℲℲℲℲℲℲℲ, ℲℲℲℲ
ℲℲℲℲℲℲℲ ℲℲℲℲℲℲℲℲℲ ℲℲℲℲℲℲℲℲℲ
ℲℲℲℲℲℲℲℲ, ℲℲℲ ℲℲ ℲℲℲℲℲℲℲ ℲℲ ℲℲℲℲ
ℲℲℲ ℲℲℲℲℲ ℲℲℲℲℲℲ,

99

Answer on Page 185

Hey, Good Looking!

The letters below will, if put together in the appropriate fashion, produce nine related words. Can you find them all? After you've found a couple of words you'll see a way to speed up your progress.

Looking!

Good

Hey

I	U	C	E	E	T	TU
O	V	S	D	T		TI
E	S	SP	G		T	TU
T	TO	O	I		G	
K	Y	O		OG		
VR		HY	R		S	E
	T	Y	E		I	
NE		W	EN			T
N		L	LN		RE	
G	N		LI	I		S

Answer on Page 185

Hide

and

Seek

In the grid you will find four boys and four girls hiding. Their name have been concealed by a simple cipher. All you have to do is find them. The words run forwards, backwards or diagonally. This puzzle is very tough at first but if you can find just one name you will get the others if you persist. In a fit of generosity I will give you the names you're seeking:

KATIE

GEORGINA

SOPHIE

BECKY

WAYNE

BENJAMIN

RICHARD

ARNOLD

```
D B N F U B M A S U W B M Q Z V I A J N
T F B A B N C T P Q N F S A D H G M D X
G H B W T I T P Q S B N T C F A Q A L Q
T S C B H M Q A L S R Q A V A P T A D W
K Y G K J C B E S C K S W Q V H I S T M
E A F R G H K W R T S P F A K D K E G N
J G E B A B Y C A P G M W T Y R P D K S
C M J I T S D A R T K I O L D S C B T I
T S D C T N O P N E F G B E M L S W A P
F B Y V E U M Z W E G J L E B W T J P B
R V B N Z A Q D R M O P G S G H J W F Y
C V M R S B Y N A R O P H S Q F K V B L
B G T C H N L D F D L O P U Q R J K D N
H K N I V O P M N G H N E B E D O K F L
N Y R H J K L E N P B F T K L D N E G N
N O E F H K G S Y L W F K A B R Y W Q L
G R V F P D D N R C Q I M D G E M A B O
F L H N M O E G O O F S B W N D H S O M
N Y T D A L N R R K M K L M B T L O D M
M O T H T R L H Y P D E L F W G D P Y N
```

Answer on Page 186

CHINESE CHALLENGE

Here's another Chinese puzzle for you. You may not realize it yet, but you already know how to solve this one. Look at it carefully and it will eventually remind you of something you did in the Easy Peasy section. Unlike the last Chinese puzzle, it would help if you were able to understand the characters but, even if you don't, you can still puzzle out what they mean. You will see that the same characters are repeated often and this should lead you to smell a rat.

三禾 　一八 　二大 　五丨

二木 　三禾 　二大 　三丨

四丨 　二木 　三丨 　一丨

一禾 　四八

Τhis is yet another well-known personage whose identity is hidden in a mass of apparently meaningless numbers. Once again the basic idea is quite simple, but it has been made more difficult by some dirty tactics intended to put you off the scent. Will you be fooled? Let's wait and see.

Bright Ideas

5	22	5	17
11	13	18	126
1	4	1	43
8	9	5	78
19	29	16	2
23	43	19	11

Answers on Page 186

Hue Hunt

In the grid you will find nine words with a common theme. Obviously the numbers are alphanumeric values but, as always, there is a twist for you to discover.

1	8	9	3
8	1	1	8
4	1	5	6
2	5	1	5
1	8	1	1
7	1	2	2
5	2	1	
2	0	2	0
1	2	5	9
1	4	2	2
1	9	1	4

2	19	8	14	18	16	13		
24	6	11	13	14	24			
15	22	17	17	11	6			
14	19	26	15	6	6			
6	13	26	22	2	16	20	20	
21	6	17	5	26	15	19		
19	22	17	18	20	16	8	19	4
21	10	14	13	4	21			
11	10	21	10	3				

Answer on Page 186

Incognito

Here we have another concealed spy. As before, you have to answer the questions before you can find the coded name. Once you have the right letters you can go to work trying to crack the code but, naturally, nothing is ever as straightforward as it looks.

Incognito

1. Bed cover

2. Associated with Thanksgiving

3. Hawaiian instrument

4. Most populous democracy on earth

5. Motown

6. Not urban

7. Vampires

8. Quantity of paper
   (sounds like singers)

9. Largest of the Pachyderms

10. Masked swordsman

Answer on Page 186

Crossword

The crossword below contains the names of numerous composers which have been encoded. Using your code-cracking abilities and your knowledge of classical music, you should be able to work out all the names.

Answer on Page 187

Incognito

Here is another hidden spy. What you have to do is answer the questions below. Each answer is a number and when you have the complete set, all you have to do is work out what the numbers stand for. A clue? You might find her among the grass.

1. One over two dozen

2. Square root of 529

3. Planets in the solar system

4. Number of cards in 2 suits

5. Signs of the Zodiac

6. Thrice half a dozen

7. Horsemen of the Apocalypse

8. Months that do not have 30 days

9. Unlucky for some

10. Passengers on a Tandem

Y ou will find six words connected with literature hidden below.

Literary Lines

EQUIP
FOREGO
GENTLE
HOMONYM
ISSUES

ENTRAP   ENTRANT
FARRIER   FAUNA
GECKO   GENIAL
HEROES   HIRSUTE
INDEPENDENCE   INNOCENTS

EXTRAS   ERUV   ELECTOR
FILLET   FORESEE   FINISH
GAZEBO   GINGER   GORY
HARRIER   HORSES   HOLOGRAM
INFAMY   INTIMATE   IMBUE

Bright Ideas

This one is really quite easy. If you find your way through it, you will discover a man famous for what he can do in spite of what he can't do.

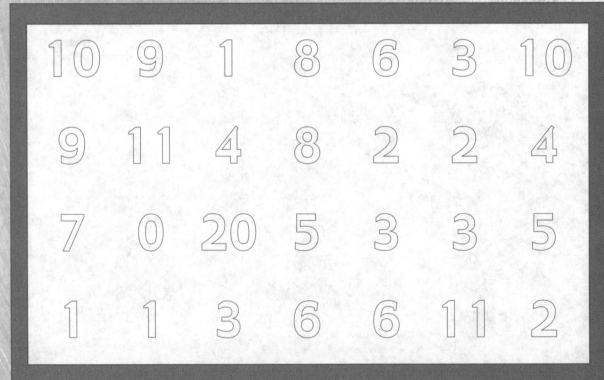

10	9	1	8	6	3	10
9	11	4	8	2	2	4
7	0	20	5	3	3	5
1	1	3	6	6	11	2

The grid below contains nine related words. With a bit of persistence they are not hard to find. When you have done a few it gets easier.

LONG JOB

5	19	19	19	5
5	21	5	18	5	1	5
6	9	12	14	9	9	12	12	19	20
14	12	5	21	14	9	1
19	5	5	5	21	14	4	19	9
21	13	12	14	4	20	14
4	14	14	2	1	15	20	3
14	3	9	14	19	9	20
22	22	19	14	5

Answers on Page 187

SNOWSEARCH

I n the grid you will find concealed the name of a Scandinavian novel that was made into a film. The only clue you have is that it has something to do with snow.

N	B	T	P	S
J	M	G	G	T
T	M	F	H	O
T	J	F	O	P
T	N	M	J	X

MADONNA MUDDLE

AIDED
ABREAST
WASPS
AIRPORT
FRESH
CORAL
BRAVE
GUITARS
THEFT
ABALONE
EYE
ROSES
SQUEALS
BED
BAKER
ABOLITION
ABOUNDING
ANGER
MOISTEN
SOLUBLE
WRESTLE
SUBMARINE
WRANGLE

If you look carefully among the words listed here, you will find a title with a connection to Madonna. The letters are not coded but have been cunningly concealed.

Answers on Page 187

Meal Muddle

This tells you of a famous location for a meal. It is doubtful that you would get served.

BLUE

ALTER

EATEN

TAPIOCA

KILOWATT

DISTAFF

ASSIMILATE

STONES

TABLET

MIASMA

Meal Muddle

TORRENT

EXTENT

IMAGO

SELF

FRANCISCAN

MYOPIA

NORMAN

JELLY

SARSAPARILLA

Answer on Page 187

Mean-Minded

Here you will discover six words, all of which are to do with bad temper. The words are, of course, concealed and it is your job to find out how they have been hidden.

BAROMETER
OBELISK
HADDOCK
FALSETTO
SAGES

SUPERFICIAL
BENFIT
HANDSOME
FRILLY
THOUSAND

TINSEL
IMPLIED
PERSECUTE
VARIETY
UKULELE

Mean-Minded

Here you will discover six words all of which are to do with bad temper. The words are, of course, concealed and it is your job to find out how they have been hidden.

TAMPER
UNDERPASS
BYEWAY
NOBLESSE
QUITTER

UNTREATED
INFLUENCED
VARIOUS
NONSENSE
QUEUE

GALLOP
JELLY
TRUST
UNIFORM
TERRITORY

Answer on Page 187

MORSE MUDDLE

As you will instantly appreciate, this puzzle is based on Morse code. If you don't know Morse, you can find it on the internet or in any number of reference books. Alternatively, ask a Boy Scout. However, as you will have already suspected, the code is only part of the problem. It will help to decode the letters but it won't give you the complete answer by a very long way. You want a clue? BALCONY. Yep, that's all you're getting.

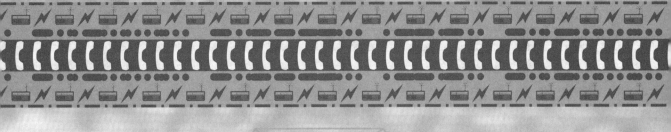

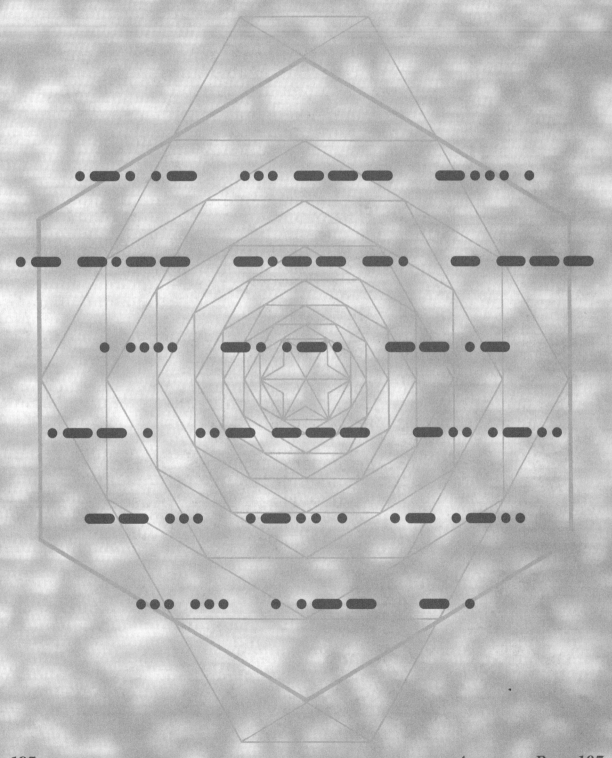

Answer on Page 187

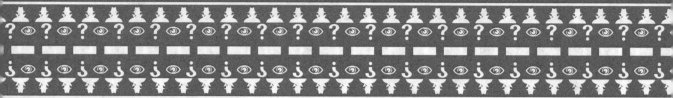

Incognito

Just how many ways can you find to hide a spy? Plenty. Here's another. The rules should be familiar by now. All you have to do is answer the questions and then you will have all the material you need to uncover the identity of our concealed agent

1. Letter that asks a question

2. Ego

3. Letter found four times in the Sundance Kid

4. The end

5. James Bond's boss

6. Roman 500

7. Heavenly twinkler

8. Legendary founders of Rome

9. Famous Italian who became a cookie

10. Sign of peace

In the grid you will find the names of six great writers. They are coded in slightly different ways. Just to show we are not completely heartless, here is a clue: they are all Americans.

6 OF THE BEST:

Writers

```
I N F M W J M M F G
F A H E Q M L D B I
N N S T R F X B Q V
J U R W K B Q S R I
O I V N A Y D G O K
H G H J C M P Q D R
X A I B N T W G P M
B J H A W L W L K H P
Z L B N S S K T P E
Q S A B N J Z D L W
```

Answers on Page 188

Morse Muddle

—•• •• —— —••   —•• •• —— ••
—•• •• —• ••••   —•• •• —— ••
—• •—• •—• —••   —••• •—• ••• ••
•—• •— ••• —••   —•• •• •—• ••—
—•• •—• •—• •••   •—— •— ••• ••

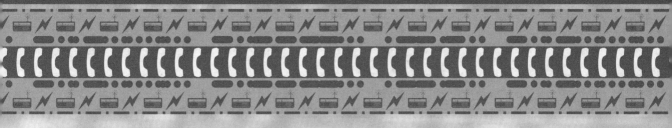

H ere is another puzzle using Morse code. Once again it will help you to work out the letters. When you have done that you should be able to see the direction this puzzle is taking.

Answer on Page 188

MOUNTAIN HIGH

Here are the names of four mountains cleverly concealed. Well, to be honest, they are not very well concealed at all. Just look carefully and you will find them.

BELIEVE
ROMANOV
SEIZE
BETTER
BECAME
KITTENS
IMPORTANT
FOOTBALLER
HONOLULU
RAMPARTS
CHURCH
ATOM
TOMATO
SURFER
CONCRETE
DISTAFF
GNU
RAJ
PASTRAMI
NOBLE
TENT
MOUNTAIN
ATLANTA

Answer on Page 188

Naming Names

Here's another group of friends cunningly concealed in a series of grids. You may have to think a while to get the trick of this one, it's not that easy. There are two tricks that you have to understand before you can find the names.

M B
O O

J O
J F

B F
L M

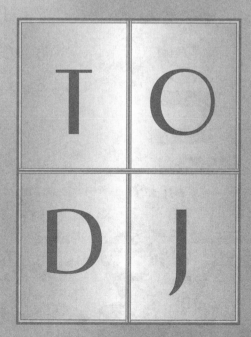
T O
D J

Answer on Page 188

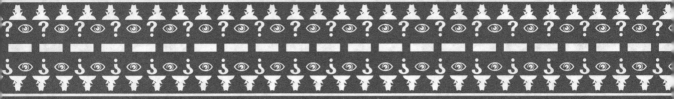

Incognito

Here is our final hidden spy. As before, all you have to do is answer the questions and then take the initial letter of each. The letters will look like a meaningless jumble until you have found out how to decode them.

1. Rude British gesture

2. The unknown

3. Composer for all seasons

4. The day of major WW2 Allied invasion

5. Sounds like waiting in line

6. Sun rises

7. US state and title of a musical

8. Castle prison cell

9. So ecomonical as to be mean

10. Apache, Cheyenne, Iroquois etc.

This is a type of puzzle you haven't tried yet. To solve it you really need a piece of information that you don't have. "That's not fair!" I hear you cry. But since when did spies play fair? Do you think the KGB stuck to the rules? The whole point of coded messages is to stop outsiders (i.e. you) from reading them. However, since this book is for fun we want you to solve the codes eventually. I'll give you a clue. The clue is: PANGRAM. If you don't know what a pangram is you'd better look it up because it is information you really need.

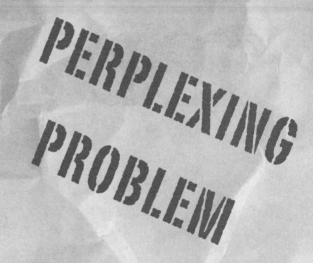

PERPLEXING PROBLEM

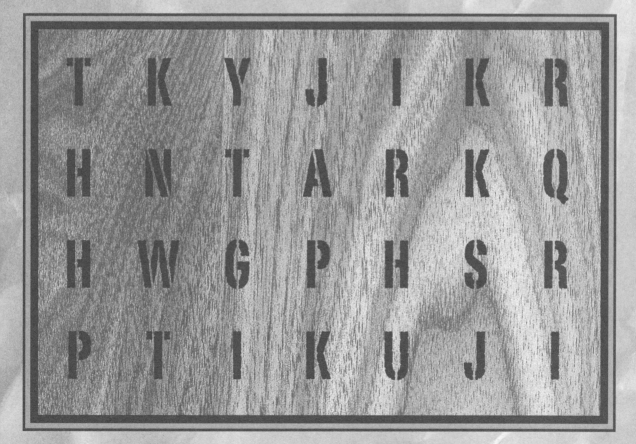

Answers on Page 188

ODD

All the groups of letters here have something in common but one of them doesn't fit the pattern. Can you tell which it is and why?

ONE

OUT

1.

C	L	A
G	O	U
A	E	T

2.

C	I	T
E	O	U
D	N	N

3.

C	O	N
T	U	R
S	E	I

4.

C	E	A
R	L	S
M	Y	O

Answer on Page 189

Riot

The letters below will, if joined up in the right way, reveal nine words that are related in meaning.

Y m e D i
N c D R H i A
H S T n o d M
d I i S u A
M o R D r I
s U A r M
S l C o
r R O D Y d
E N O f d A
i A e E n u

T he letters below are accompanied, as you can see, by various symbols. The question you must ask yourself is, "What do the symbols mean?". Once you have the answer you will be able to find the name of an American president concealed within the verbiage.

SY∏B⊕LIC

Its ayy ypeek to µe

A - M % G § A § I § F %

K µ S ® B % D - N Ω T §

L - T µ N ® & µ G ® L -

G § Q - E § M µ N § A ®

E Σ Q % P ® S § O ® C %

F - O § I µ U ® M µ O §

B % P % W § A - G § L -

E § D ® S % B % P % E ®

U ® R § L - H § C Σ N §

Answer on Page 189

NORSE

NONSENSE

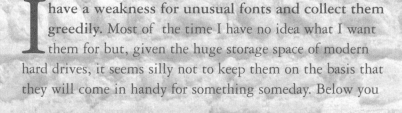

I have a weakness for unusual fonts and collect them greedily. Most of the time I have no idea what I want them for but, given the huge storage space of modern hard drives, it seems silly not to keep them on the basis that they will come in handy for something someday. Below you will find text set in a Norse script. All you have to do is turn it back into English. Naturally nothing is ever as straightforward as it might seem and though you will soon start to work out the English equivalents of the Pictish letters, you may have a surprise in store.

NORSE

NONSENSE

Answer on Page 189

6 OF THE BEST:

Detectives

Below you will find six famous detectives in disguise. They are not easy to spot so you will have to stimulate the little grey cells (clue!) before you try. All the names have been coded in the same way so, when you've got one, getting the rest should be reasonably easy.

```
Q P J S P U D C D V
G B A Q L S Z I M O
I P M N F T G J P P
A D S E G N L O V F
L K D O X Z A C T H
N B S Q M F H K F P
D P M V N C P L B T
M B T U S N I P V U
F W L M A U K D C O
J S P M T J E F E G
```

PRESIDENT PROBLEM

Midnight
Ajar
Groan
Pendulous
Cheep
Anthem
Arapaho

Left
Affable
Brown
Galoshes
Painfully
Abrade
Pizzazz

Unusual
Aspen
Invert
Bring
Kebab
Adagio

The names of some US presidents are concealed in the words on the left. See if you can find them.

141

Shy

Singer

A shy singer has taken refuge in the crowd below. Can you find her? She isn't normally shy; in fact the word flamboyant would be more appropriate.

11
24
4   11
15   10
15   21
12   4

5 12 15 15 28 5 18 5 23 11 18 21 17 23 18 17

4   4   15   23
21   12
5   25
21   8
4   21
22   22
23   23
21   22   18
8 15 4 19 12 8 6   17
22   18   8 15 15 8 16 6 19 11 8 21 22 18 17
4   18
17   5
7   28
    7
    18
    18

Answer on Page 189

RIVER
DEEP
DEEP
RIVER

Here you will find the names of four famous rivers of the world. They have all been encoded in the same way. The code is not at all subtle. In fact, the answers are staring you right in the face. Can you work out how to crack this code? It is not nearly as hard as you might think.

MATTER	AEON	ASSETS
CHAIN	ATTACK	ASPHYXIA
ABLE	UTAH	GAINING
MEDIAEVAL	ISAAC	ASTRAL
ARTFUL	AMERICA	PASSION
ASSENT	AERONAUT	MAINTAIN
ENCYCLOPAEDIA	ASPIDISTRA	APPRENTICE
MAINTAIN	AMSTERDAM	APPLAUD
BLAND	RAIN	UNCERTAIN

Answer on Page 189

THE ROSICRUCIAN CODE

The Rosicrucians grew out of the confluence of alchemists, Christian Kabbalists and religious reformers that swept through Europe in the 1500s as a result of the spread of the printing press. The information explosion that spread a mystical Christianity and brought enlightenment to many scholars also brought these men into contact with one another. The English mystic and alchemist Dr John Dee travelled through Europe for six years, widely disseminating his alchemical tract called the Monas Hieroglyphica.

The rose had long been an alchemical symbol of the great work of spiritual transformation, and the rose was also a symbol of silence concerning secret knowledge; thus, the rose was carved on the ceilings of meeting places to symbolize this, giving us the term 'sub-rosa'. The cross was an alchemical symbol of the material world and also symbolized salvation to the alchemists, most of whom were also Christians. The combination of these symbols was an alchemical device used to symbolize the opening of spiritual consciousness in one whose consciousness was based in the physical world.

Exactly what the Rosicrucians did is a matter of much debate. Some whose active imaginations exceed their knowledge credit this secret society with all sorts of mysterious powers. It has even been claimed that they were the custodians of the Holy Grail. The truth is that though there is a mass of information about this movement much of it is misleading and many of the 'facts' are hotly disputed by historians. But what we do know is that the Rosicrucians tried to maintain their secrecy by writing in code.

There is more than one Rosicrucian code but the one we have used has gained wide currency (although some deny it was anything to do with the Rosicrucians and claim that it was actually invented during the American Civil War.) If it is true that the Rosicrucians tried to hide their secrets with this particular code then they were doomed to disappointment. The code is not especially difficult to crack. Once you have an inkling of how it is constructed it will take you only a matter of minutes to break it.

Answer on Page 190

ODD

One of these groups of letters is the odd one out. Which is it and why?

ONE

OUT

1.

C G E
S W S
N A O

2.

A N D
H B G
T R V

3.

H G A
O K B
L E I

4.

B F J
O T U
F J O

149

Answer on Page 190

Stupid Perhaps?

This should keep you guessing for a while. The answer is a single word. You need a clue? No you don't (and that *is* a clue!).

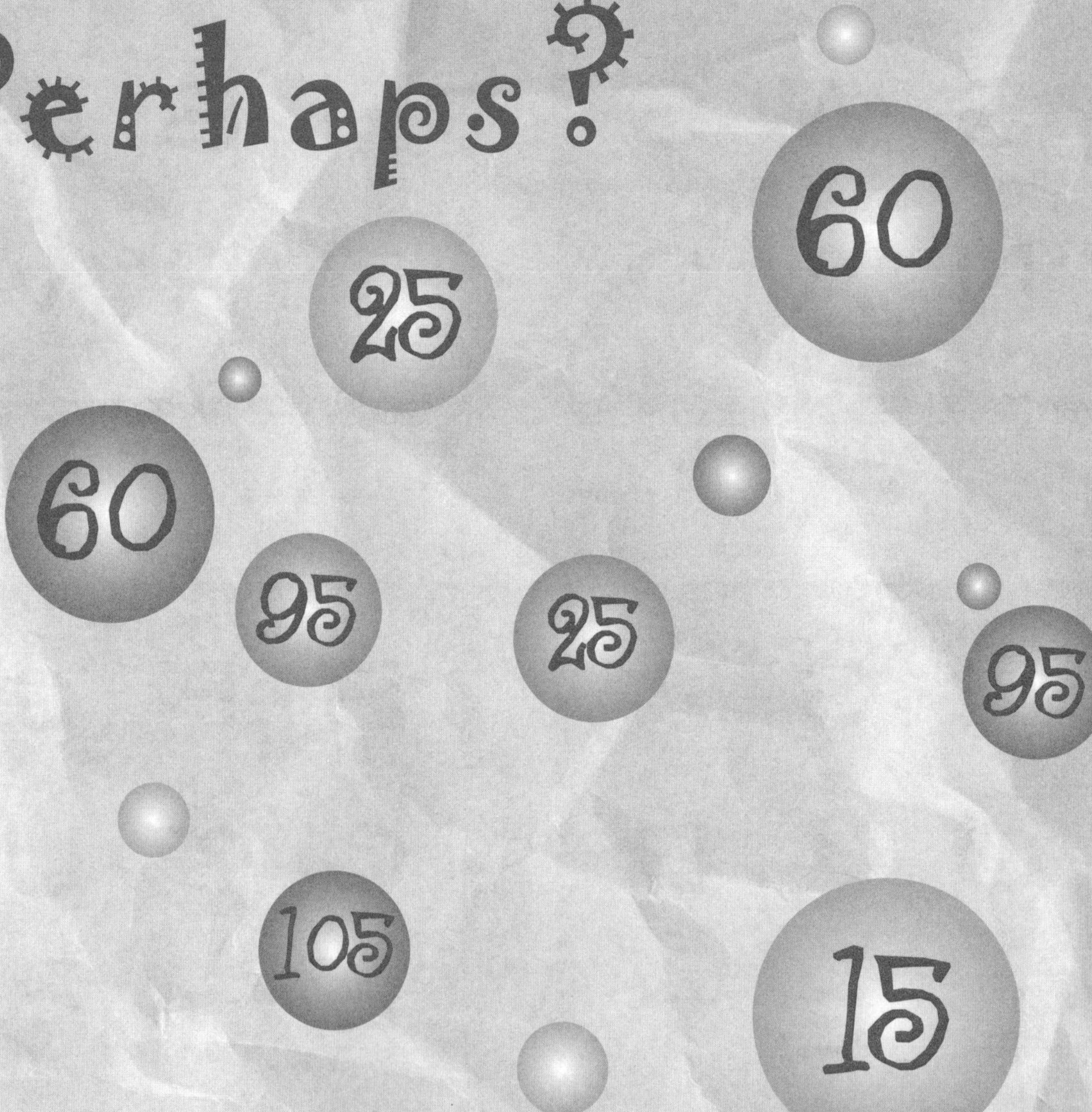

60

25

60

95

25

95

105

15

Strangely there are not that many women who were so famous as to be known by only one name. A few lists appear on the internet but they are rather eccentric (one of them includes Beyoncé but omits one of the most famous women who ever lived). See who you can find concealed below. As before, they have been encoded in slightly different ways.

6 OF THE BEST:

Women

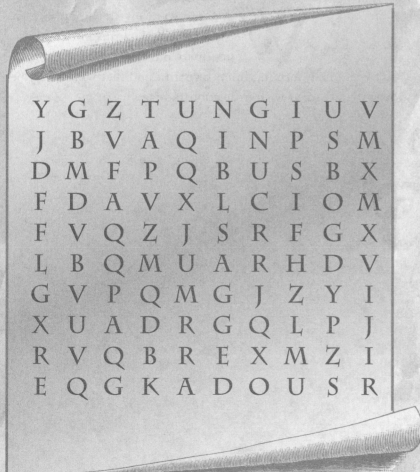

```
Y G Z T U N G I U V
J B V A Q I N P S M
D M F P Q B U S B X
F D A V X L C I O M
F V Q Z J S R F G X
L B Q M U A R H D V
G V P Q M G J Z Y I
X U A D R G Q L P J
R V Q B R E X M Z I
E Q G K A D O U S R
```

Answer on Page 190

SILLY SEMAPHORE

What can we do with semaphore to squeeze a little amusement from its dusty old flags? Ah ha! An idea is forming in my twisted mind that will drive you mad with frustration and rage

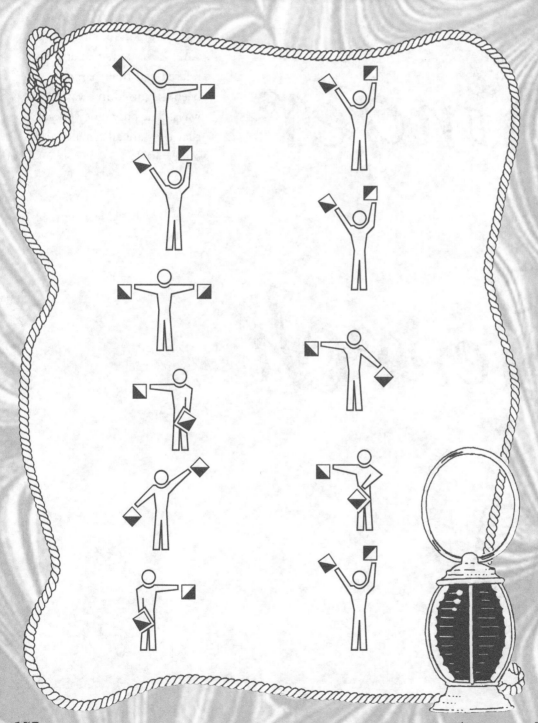

Answer on Page 190

Singer

Search

H ere are the names of six singers. They are not in any way related and their names have been disguised in a variety of ways. The only clue you get is that they are all females and under 30

51 34 50 40 36 50 19 46 80 21 36 12
50 12 32 31 24 38 18 24 71 14 22 7

2 5 3 1 4 2 5 14 1 19
7 3 6 1 2 5 3 1 5 1

10 15 19 19 19 20 15 14 5
8 13 22 4 18 13 5 7 3

22 9 40 13 10 34 10 32 42 18
18 2 26 18 14 26 16 24 23 2

1 100 125 300 60 96 4 58 195 41 250 9
0 69 500 229 21 100 21 6 30 400 111 16

12 24 36 43 3 99 45 16 12 28 63 44
19 15 8 60 16 21 86 45 7 54 31 39

Answer on Page 190

SQUARE MEAL

The words here conceal six other words all to do with food. How do you find them?

ASPEN
PSEUDO
IGLOO
ABROAD
CHURCH

RAFT
BARREL
ACCORDION
FLOUT
CONCUR

STABBING
CREEK
AVIARY
GONE
USHER

CONSTABLE

REACHING

FORMIC

BLOOD

GROUND

TRAPPED

EIDER

QUIZ

DOZED

EQUAL

APPLES

BEACHED

ISOTOPE

OTTER

PERSUADE

Answer on Page 190

ODD

One of these groups of numbers is unlike the others. Which one is it and why?

ONE

OUT

1.

1	13	4
0	6	4
1	18	8

2.

11	12	13
9	12	11
20	24	24

3.

8	6	1
14	13	1
22	19	2

4.

15	10	3
6	11	8
21	26	11

Answer on Page 190

Once again there is a connection between the symbols and letters. Work out what it is and you will discover the name of someone as famous for his death as for his life.

°SYΠBΘLIC

^†ßå¬¬©®´¨°†øµe

B	∂	L	¬	V	#	R	∂	I	∂
A	§	J	Ω	S	#	A	§	S	§
F	∂	N	∂	U	Ω	L	Ω	I	Ω
J	#	J	§	J	§	A	#	D	#
U	Ω	I	¬	E	∂	T	¬	A	¬
N	¬	S	Ω	P	µ	E	§	C	Ω
I	§	O	#	C	¬	A	Ω	W	§
U	µ	U	µ	E	Ω	L	µ	A	∂
S	Ω	A	Ω	N	µ	Q	∂	R	§
P	¬	A	§	O	§	N	#	R	Ω

160

SYMBOLIC

Here is another symbol puzzle. This time the challenge is to find a villain famous for his falsely avuncular manner. He lurks somewhere below and the only indication of his presence is found through careful examination of the symbols.

H Ω	A !	H !	R ¬	B #	
A §	N Ω	G §	K #	L §	
N !	M #	P #	P Ω	K Ω	
B #	C ¬	E ®	A ¬	A ®	
D ®	T !	P !	E !	O !	
I !	A §	S ®	N §	N #	
V ®	O ®	B Ω	M §	X ¬	
E Ω	E #	E ¬	G #	W Ω	
I §	R ®	L ¬	F Ω	J !	
L !	S !	O #	S !	S ¬	

Answers on Pages 190 & 191

ODD

L ook at the groups of numbers here and see if you can spot which one is unlike the others.

ONE

OUT

1.

26	25	19
12	9	9
22	13	7

2.

26	25	12
9	18	20
18	13	22

3.

26	13	26
15	20	22
8	18	24

4.

14	25	5
24	12	22
13	26	7

Answer on Page 191

SYMBOLIC

There is no end to the ingenious ways in which information can be hidden in a table of symbols and letters. Here's another problem for you to grapple with. Of course, the difficulty will be of a sort you have not encountered before. When you have worked out the relationship between symbols and letters you will discover a singer also known for her acting.

ονε μορε σψμβολιχ πυζζλε το γο

C	æ	C	Œ	G	≠	L	¬	E	≠
N	¬	Z	≠	W	¬	D	¬	A	¬
A	Œ	A	¬	Q	Œ	F	≠	C	¬
E	¬	V	¬	F	é	E	æ	U	≠
D	¬	O	¬	H	æ	R	æ	B	¬
S	≠	E	¬	M	≠	G	¬	P	é
Q	¬	P	é	P	¬	J	¬	T	é
B	¬	R	≠	S	é	E	≠	X	¬
L	≠	N	¬	E	¬	Y	¬	A	Œ
A	¬	P	é	O	¬	L	¬	C	≠

This puzzle is all about military might. The men below are all known for the enthusiasm with which they set out to conquer the world. Some are considered heroes and others villains. Some started out as heroes but became villains as their careers progressed. Can you find them?

6 OF THE BEST:

Conquerors

```
C A V I B A X E D O
Q L V L M X P I V K
E O K P F M O N T A
L G E B Y R T X A J
Q M R D B J S Y K L
E G Z Z O R G F V H
A L J A E F P Q A L
C D Q M F S D N E H
V R E T S P I S R K
B H R V L K J Q H J
```

Answers on Page 191

6 OF THE BEST –

Roman Emperors

In the grid you will discover the names of six Roman emperors. To add interest to the puzzle the names have been encoded in slightly different ways so, just because you have one, it doesn't mean you'll find the others.

```
K C V E K A L D E M X
U J C F S J V T Y X
O V F L O I D U K O
U M R P T A S N Y L
F C M G A R Y S W X
G G I T V W N Z X V
B Q D Q A T V B Y X
N B Y T N O A S W C
A H F Q N L Z Q F N
R F O D X G L X V B
```

Look carefully at the following mixture of signs and letters. If you can uncover the correct relationship between them, you will reveal the name of a cartoon character famous for his healthy eating habits.

this is the γλοι αμβφοιΥ πηζζγε

SYMBOLIC

B Σ L * R + I ¬ U % H *
V + I Σ S ∂ T * R ∂ V Σ
N & B % O & L % G ¬ A ∂
U % U * C + U ∂ N ∂ R *
M + N + M & S Σ L % C ¬
O Σ T % K % C ¬ Q ¬ W ∂
A ∂ F ¬ L ∂ R % N ∂ G *
G % L * D + N ∂ D ¬ M #
S & B + B % Y * X % I #
H ∂ A ∂ G & E ¬ Y # Y *

Answer on Page 191

THE NAME GAME

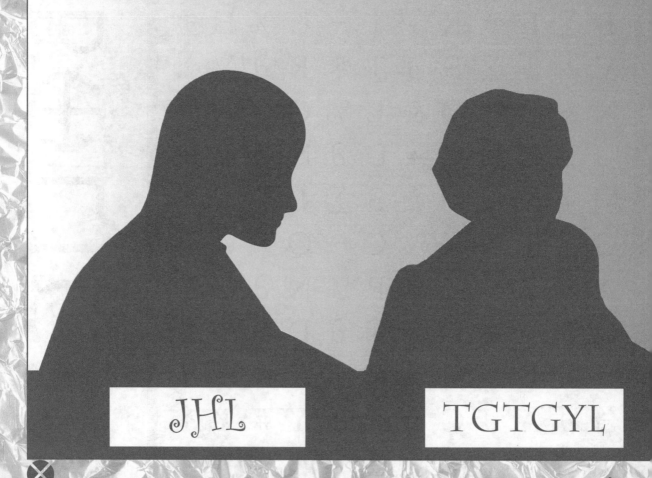

JHL   TGTGYL

This one is really quite simple but it might cause you to scratch your head a bit. It is really a simple deciphering job but with, as always, an added complication. The challenge is to be flexible enough in your thinking to catch on to the sneaky trick that is being played on you. OK, enough intro, the task that faces you is this: which one of the people below is a woman?

YLYYV   FQJA

Answer on Page 191

Veiled Villain

There is a movie bad guy lurking in the verbal undergrowth ready to pounce. You can also find the name of the actor who plays him.

ABHOR
SMACK
BRAVE
PANIC
SPANNER
WITCH
WHIST
ASHEN
DOUBLED
FRONT
BRAKE
VAUNTED
SILLY
EYE

UNCLASP
ACHED
TREAT
GLOVE
YUCCA
IMPLY
INTER
ASKED
MIMETIC
ABOMINATE
FORAY
ANT
ACCOSTING

There are five famous writers concealed below. See if you can find them.

WRITER RIDDLE

```
D M C L E O U
K I R R U N N
K E E R I A S
E I O O E A G
T H P K S N C
```

Answers on Pages 191 & 192

Wild Goose Chase

The grid may look as if it is full of a meaningless jumble of letters. That's because it is - except for one line which contains the phrase "wild goose chase". Naturally the phrase is in code and your job is to find it. The code itself is very simple, but even so finding it will prove something of a challenge. However, if you're clever you can work out that some of the columns and rows could not possibly be correct. That will narrow your search considerably.

```
V B M K T G G S P N D V X X
B G D H C T K C L A U I J O
B N S H E V V L B X A R M T
J F O Y W C M L J F N B E N
D A Q W E R G H K L A A H C
Q W E R T Y U I O P A S P F
Q B H F C B K J T M N B P S
V J R O V G E T R W I H T V
B G Y O R T J D A W H D F L
A D T Y F E W V F E R T D B
D M H Y A R T O X U G T I N
W V D Y T I O N M W T T B N
F H Y R T A W S F T G Y T V
V G H T N U O S F E G J F K
```

SILLY SEMAPHORE

Let's see if we can have a bit more fun with semaphore before consigning it once again to the lumber room of history. You can either do this the hard way or you can look up the semaphore alphabet and see how much good that does. Of course, I am going to make things as hard as possible, but then if it were easy anyone could do it.

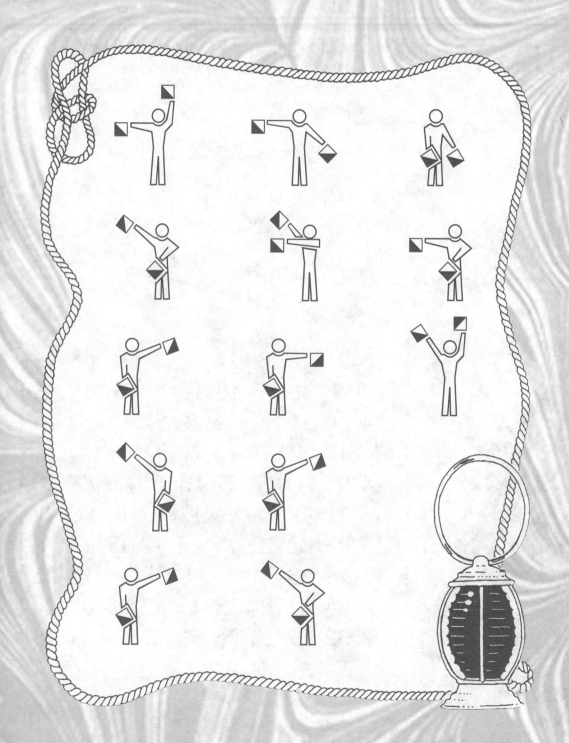

Answer on Page 192

6 OF THE BEST:

In the grid you will find six musical performers (five bands and one solo artist). They have been hidden in various ways. Beware – some of them turn corners!

Musical performers

10	21	8	8	17	7	4	28	65	13
22	7	26	53	18	14	9	6	49	12
24	26	11	39	24	8	87	18	10	16
5	45	12	21	42	17	23	15	10	16
24	93	20	8	37	10	14	7	88	28
6	11	8	18	84	12	10	19	90	8
17	43	22	12	99	25	97	15	24	4
12	18	23	21	8	4	56	4	18	23
4	25	21	12	15	15	32	28	86	26
5	82	19	23	76	30	7	15	21	18

```
A T F V S Y N I Z H
I M L Z T K K T A Y
L C E K F Z Z P Y H
Y X V A X E Y K M Z
Z W Y V K A E N E A
E N N W O T X L X X
F I A F L I F M F F
R A Z H Z M W U W N
T V E K W H H K H A
H F V X M L V N V E
```

Where is the body buried?

Somewhere in the grid a body lies. It is not actually hidden - in fact you can see it quite clearly, but you may still be unable to find it. See if you can spot where it has been put.

Answers on Page 192

BAR CODE

Pete's girlfriend had just dumped him so he went to a bar to drown his sorrows. For a while he sat staring moodily at the bottles lined up behind the bar. After a while he had a sudden thought. He pulled out his pocket diary and began to scribble. After a few minutes he smiled and spoke to the barman. What did he say?

Estate
Waterfall
Lapidary
Effrontery
Rustic
Eastern
Natural
Zenith
Radish
Earthenware
Gargoyle
Electric
Legitimate
Evanescent

Confused

actress

Concealed in this list is the name of a well-known actress who found fame when she took drastic steps to conceal her own identity in a various ways. Can you find her? You'd like a clue? She isn't British but is at home in London.

Answers on Page 192

Answers Answers Answe

001 – EASY PEASY

This is easy to read when you know how…

	A	B	C	D	E	F	G	H	I
1	C	F	J	M	P	S	V	Y	Z
2	B	E	I	L	O	R	U	X	
3	A	D	H	K	N	Q	T	W	

002 – EASY PEASY

To be or not to be that is the question.

The sentence was simply typed out and converted to a font called Wingdings (which you probably have on your computer).

003 – MORSE MUDDLE

I left my heart in San Francisco. (Song title)

As you now see the Morse Code was merely a cover for some fairly simple anagrams. The hard bit was working out where the word breaks came.

004 – DARK STORY

The text comes from the opening lines of Homer's *Iliad*. Each letter has been swapped for the one before it in the alphabet. It begins, *"An angry man – there is my story…"*

005 – A GOOD-HUMOURED PUZZLE

The letters A, B, C, D, E appeat in each of the words. The letters following these form the words you are looking for. They are: *Laugh, Mirth, Merry, Happy, Funny, Sunny.*

006 – 6 OF THE BEST: BIBLICAL CHARACTERS

The six names are: *Samuel, Malachi, Ezekiel, Daniel, Jeremiah, Isiah.*

All the names have been moved several places in the alphabet

							N	P
I		U		K		N	I	D
F		C		D		V	V	O
S		O		L		I	I	D
N		W		D		Q	Q	F
J		G		V		M	M	K
Q		N		L		E	E	L
							L	
	I	D	I	O	M	I	P	

007 – A LITTLE ALCHEMY

The passage comes from the introduction to *The Golden Ass* by Apuleius. Here's the English version:

If you are not put off by the Egyptian storytelling convention which allows humans to be changed into animals and, after various adventures, restored to their proper shapes, you should be amused by this queer novel, a string of anecdotes in the Miesian style but intended only for your private ear, which I call my "Transformations".

008 – A WRITE MUDDLE

The names are written backwards with the vowels removed.

Harper Lee – *To Kill a Mockingbird*
Douglas Adams – *The Hitchhiker's Guide to the Galaxy*
Henry Fielding – *Tom Jones*
Margaret Mitchell – *Gone with the Wind*

Answers Answers Ansr

009 – BRIGHT IDEAS

If you take the first and last letters of alternate lines you get the name *Einstein*.

010 – A PLACE OF ONE'S OWN

If you take the last letter of each word you wil find that the following ore spelled backwards: *Lodge, Tents, House, Tepee, Igloo, Homes.*

011 – ABSENT FRIENDS?

The names were hardly disguised at all. Their letters were simply mixed up in pairs.
Dave, Mary – Dick, Jane (or Jean) – Sean, Kate

012 – BLIND LOGIC

From Romeo and Juliet: *"O, She doth teach the torches to burn bright."*

013 – ARTFULLY CONCEALED

The names are formed from the inital letters of the words read from bottom to top. They are: *Turner, Picasso, Monet.*

014 – AMEN CORNER

All the words are symmetrical. Take the middle letter and use the one that comes before it in alphabetical order. This gives: *Altar, Prays, Kneel, Bible, Hymns, Bless.*

015 – CIRCULAR CONUNDRUM

The letters are turned into their alphanumeric values. Count every third letter, the others being nonsense. The book title is: *To Kill a Mockingbird.*

016 – HIDDEN ADVENTURER

If you take the letters that are common to two words, you will find that you can spell out *Lara Croft*

017 – BLIND LOGIC

In Braille the letters A–J can also be used as numerals (though when you start to use numbers there is a special sign you should include to show what you're doing). The letters in the puzzle have been expressed as numbers based on their alphabetic position (A = 1, Z = 26). The answer is: *Lithuania.*

018 – BRIGHT IDEAS

It is a simple word scramble. All the letters are there in a jumbled order. Unscrambled they spell: *Leonardo Da Vinci*

019 – CARD CAPERS

Hearts and Diamonds stand for letters. The Spades and Clubs are merely a distraction.

Hearts		Diamonds	
A	Ace of Hearts	N	Ace of Diamonds
B	2 of Hearts	O	2 of Diamonds
C	3 of Hearts	P	3 of Diamonds
D	4 of Hearts	Q	4 of Diamonds
E	5 of Hearts	R	5 of Diamonds
F	6 of Hearts	S	6 of Diamonds
D	7 of Hearts	T	7 of Diamonds
H	8 of Hearts	U	8 of Diamonds
I	9 of Hearts	V	9 of Diamonds
J	10 of Hearts	W	10 of Diamonds
K	Jack of Hearts	X	Jack of Diamonds
L	Queen of Hearts	Y	Queen of Diamonds
M	King of Hearts	Z	King of Diamonds

The cryptogram reads: *"Now is the Winter of our discontent".*

Answers Answers Answ

020 – HIDDEN HEROINES

Keira Knightly and *Parminder Nagra*. Keira was in *Pirates of the Carribean* and Parminder appears in *ER*. They both appeard in *Bend it Like Beckham*.

021 – CHINESE CHALLENGE

The characters correspond to English letters by the number of strokes in them (one stroke = A, two = B, three = C, etc). This works until you get to M but the characters become too complicated (and the maximum number of strokes is only about 22). So for M, I went back to the beginning and AA = M, BB = N, CC = O, etc. The whole thing reads: *"Here is the story of Goldilocks and the three bears."*

022 – CASH CRISIS

Take the first letter of each of the given words and move three places backwards in the alphabet. This gives: *Money, Dough, Bucks, Cents, Spend, Dimes.*

023 – CD DILEMMA

The letters are represented by their alphanumeric values, which have been doubled. The band names are: *Queen, Rolling Stones, Green Day, Razor Light, Dire Straits, Beatles.*

024 – CONCEALED COMPOSERS

The names are formed from the mixed-up final letters of the words. They are: *Beethoven, Mozart, Borodin.*

025 – CONCEALED CROOK

The shared letters are T, D, B, S, G, B, D, F. If you move them all one place up the alphabetical order, you will get the letters to make *Scarface*.

026 – CROSSWORD

027 – CARD CAPERS

The cards have the same values as in previous Card Capers, but all the vowels are represented by the Jack of Clubs and the cards are laid out in reverse order. The cryptogram reads: *"Once upon a time there was a girl named Snow White"*.

Answers Answers Answ

028 – CRYPTO WORDSEARCH

Julia Roberts = *KVMJB SPCFSUT*

Robert Redford = *QNADQS QDCENQC*

Colin Firth = *DPMJO GJSUI*

Hugh Grant = *GTFI HSBOU*

Ashley Olson = *BTIMFZ PMTPO*

Brad Pitt = *CSBE QJUU*

Angelina Jolie = *BOEFMJOB KPMJF*

Cameron Diaz = *DBNFSPO EJBA*

Halle Berry = *IBMMF CFSSZ*

Liam Neeson = *MJBN MFFTPO*

Donald Sutherland = *EPMBME TVUIFSMBME*

Pierce Brosnan = *QJFSDF CSPTMBM*

```
B G H T E O P S D E J U P L M N W T S F
C F R T H G X W Y U O I P L K J N F T M
V T R S Q B G T N H Y O P I L K J M N Y
C T Y H G E U Y I O P B B M H S W R E T S
V G T I U Y B B M H S W R E T D G T D W
S G T Y H A S E T O B K N S E R T Y N M
V Q R T Y B F W C F G N Y T A S D E F J
C N E F T Q J F S D F C S P T M B M B N
E A C D C V R T S U J Y M F P O W G T H O N M
C D C V R T S H G W U Y F T E T H O O F
X Q S Z E M O W Q W D E G T Y H Y U O F
D S B E A D K V M B J S P C F S U T U O
B Q E V T M O P L K Q T E U T U I O P
N D Q B T Y U P X E D R T O P B Q W G P
F C E J B A S E R T G Y T Y U I T T N O
S E U Y A X C T W U T R B O N I W D M
P N Q U T V R T N A S W N Y P R M V T I
O Q C E V T R Y U I M Y W E F E S H T
E C S D P M I O G J S U I C R Z E V S C
J Z I O C E B T Y H B Y I O P P W V B N
B A W D E R G Y T O I D F E B T M T O U Y
A C E T R Q P O I B G T Y O I T R E U Y
C E R I B M M F C F S S Z B T P B T Y
V R G T F H N B N Y D E T T R O V R R
T F T T W Y R G R O P T E W N H W T T
R Y T Y D N E B O E F M J O B K P M J F
E R G P T O G V R T Y E O P B T B T P V
G E P M B M E T V U I F S M B M E X W T
T W W V P H Q D R T Y N H Y E D R F T
N E R B T I M F Z P M T R O C Y E O U P
```

029 – DANCE DILEMMA

The letters L, M, N, O P appear in that order in each set of words. The letter following one of these is the one you need. Put together they give: *Dance, Music, Polka, Waltz, Rumba, Salsa.*

030 – DEAF WORDS

Sign language solution: *The quick brown fox jumps over the lazy dog.*

031 – CHINESE CHALLENGE

Solution: *To be attacked by the enemy is not a bad thing but a good thing.*

	一	二	三	四	五
丿	A	B	C	D	E
亻	F	G	H	IJ	K
大	L	M	N	O	P
木	Q	R	S	T	U
禾	V	W	X	Y	Z

032 – DEAF WORDS

Z represents A, Y represents B and so on: *a bright sunny day in the depths of winter.*

033 – HONOURABLE SPEECH

The speech is Mark Antony's funeral oration at Caesar's funeral. It starts in the middle and winds outwards in a spiral. The alphabet has been divided into five-letter sections which are numbered alternately forwards and backwards. It reads: *Friends, Romans, Countrymen lend me your ears. I come to bury caesar not to praise him.*

034 – HOUSE HUNTING

This one is really very easy. The letters are simply moved on one in the alphabet. The *US President* goes in the *White House*, the *British PM* goes to *Downing Street*, the *Pope* in the *Vatican* and the *Russion leader* is found in the *Kremlin*.

035 – BLIND LOGIC

The Braille signs have been turned upside down and flipped over. The answer is the book title, *The Cruel Sea*.

036 – LONG JOURNEY

Mr Phileas Fogg lived in Saville Row, Burlington gardens, the house where Sheridan died. He was one of the most noticeable members of the Reform Club, though he seemed always to avoid attracting attention; in an enigmatical personage, about whom little was known except that he was a polished man of the world. People said that he resembled Byron – at least that his head was Byronic; but he was a bearded, tranquil Byron, who might live on a thousand years without growing old.

Certainly an Englishman, I was more doubtful whether Fogg was a Londoner. He was never seen on 'Change, not at the Bank, nor in the counting rooms of the 'City'; no ships ever came into London docks of which he was the owner; he had no public employment; he had never been entered at any of the Inns of Court, or Gray's Inn, nor had his voice ever resounded in the Court of Chancery.

037 – FIND THE LADY

Take the first and last letters of the words alternately. The answer is: *Statue of Liberty*

038 – CROSSWORD

The code is just Zapf dingbats.

039 – CARD CAPERS

It was the day my grandmother exploded. This is the opening line from *The Crow Road* by Iain Banks (if you haven't read it you really should). As you have no doubt guessed by this time, I turned it into cards by the normal method but then complicated matters by using a Caesar's substitution code in which A=G and Z=F.

Answers Answers Ansr

040 – CROSSWORD

041 – SILLY SEMAPHORE

Kiss me, Hardy. Reportedly the last words of Admiral Nelson.

042 – INCOGNITO

The answers to the questions are: 1. *Janus*, 2. *Valentine*, 3. *Kentucky*, 4. *Oglala*, 5. *Union*, 6. *Parasol*, 7. *Quito*, 8. *Omerta*, 9. *Kilo*, 10. *Umber*. The name you are looking for is *Simon Smith*. It is spelled backwards and the letters have been moved two places down the alphabet.

043 – DEAF WORDS

Numbers refer to the keypad on a cell phone. The sentence reads: *If music be the food of love, play on.*

044 – EASY PEASY

The text is actually the first sentence of the introduction but it has been written backwards and the letters broken up into small groups. It reads; *People make the mistake of assuming that codes have to be complicated whereas, in fact, even very simple devices can cause the solver problems.*

045 – FOR A RAINY AFTERNOON

The text is, as you may have realized by now, in Latin. The original (written by Pliny) looks like this: *Formam eius in speciem orbis absoluti globatam esse nomen in primis et consensus in eo mortalium orbem appellantium, sed et argumenta rerum docent, non solum quia talis figura omnibus sui partibus vergit in sese ac sibi ipsa toleranda est seque includit et continet nullarum egens compagium nec finem aut initium ullis sui partibus sentiens, nec quia ad motum, quo subinde verti mox adparebit, talis aptissima est, sed oculorum quoque probatione, quod convexu mediusque quacumque cernatur, cum id accidere in alia non possit figura,*

046 – HEY, GOOD LOOKING!

Always using the fonts in the same order you'll get:

PRETTY
LOVELY
DIVINE
CUTE
SWEET
GORGEOUS
STRIKING
STUNNING
HOT

Answers Answers Answe

047 – HIDE AND SEEK

```
D B N F U B M A S U W B M Q Z V G A J N
T F B A B N A R N O L D S A D H E M D X
G H B W I T P Q S B N T C F A O K L Q
R S C B H M Q A L S R Q A V P K V A D
I Y G K J C B E S C K S W Q V H G S T M
C A F R G H K W R T S P F A K D I E G N
H G E B A B W A Y N E M W T Y R N D K S
A M J I T S D A R T K I O L D S A B T I
R S D C T N O P N E F G B E M L S W A P
D B Y V E U M Z W E G J L E B W T J P B
R V B N Z A Q D R M O P G S G H J W F Y
C V K R S B Y N A R O P H S Q F K V B L
B G T A H N L D F B L O P S O P H I E N
H K N I T O P M N E H N E B E D O K F L
N Y R H J I L E N N B F T K L D N E G N
N O E F H K E S Y J W F K A B R Y W Q L
G R V F P D D N R A Q I M B E C K Y B O
F L H N M O E G O M F S B W N D H S O M
N Y T D A L N R R I M K L M B T L O D M
M O T H T R L H Y N D E L F W G D P Y N
```

048 – CHINESE CHALLENGE

It's actually the beginning of Queen's *Bohemian Rhapsody* (*Is this the real life, is this just fantasy?*). As you can see, it is just a grid code hiding itself behind Chinese fancy dress.

	木	丿	冫	禾	大
二	A	B	C	D	E
—	F	G	H	IJ	K
囚	L	M	N	O	P
三	Q	R	S	T	U
五	V	W	X	Y	Z

049 – BRIGHT IDEAS

The letters are represented by their alphanumeric values. They run up the first and third columns from bottom to top. All the other numbers are distracters with the large numbers being included to put you off the scent of the alphanumeric values. The name you're looking for is: *W. Shakespeare*.

050 – HUE HUNT

The alphanumeric values are always one place out but they alternate so that they are one place before or one place after the true value.

C	R	I	M	S	O	N		
Y	E	L	L	O	W			
P	U	R	P	L	E			
O	R	A	N	G	E			
G	L	A	U	C	O	U	S	
V	E	R	D	A	N	T		
T	U	R	Q	U	O	I	S	E
V	I	O	L	E	T			
L	I	V	I	D				

051 – INCOGNITO

The answers to the questions are: 1. *Quilt*, 2. *November*, 3. *Ukulele*, 4. *India*, 5. *Detroit*, 6. *Rural*, 7. *Undead*, 8. *Quire*, 9. *Elephant*, 10. *Zorro*. The name you are looking for is *Frank Brown*. As you will have realized, the letters are jumbled. I did say it wasn't straightforward, didn't I? The initial letters have been moved three places in the alphabet.

AnswersAnswersAnsw

052 – CROSSWORD

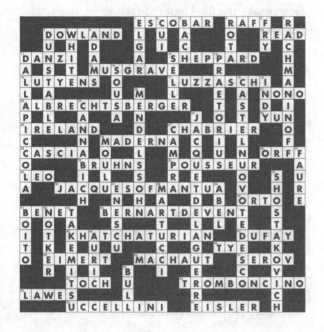

053 – INCOGNITO

The name is *Daisy Brown*. The numbers (which are jumbled) correspond to the correct letters if the alphabet is numbered backwards. The answers to the questions are: 1. *25=B*, 2. *23=D*, 3. *9=R*, 4. *26=A*, 5. *12=0*, 6. *18=I*, 7. *4=W*, 8. *8=S*, 9. *13=N*, 10. *2=Y*.

054 – LITERARY LINES

The final letters of each word give: *Poems, Prose, Story, Tales, Verse, Rhyme.*

055 – BRIGHT IDEAS

The numbers are added to get their alphanumeric values. The top two rows give *Stephen* and the bottom two give *Hawking*.

056 – LONG JOB

The numbers are alphanumeric values. The fonts are always used in the same order. The words are: *Endless, Infinite, Unending, Eternal, Vast, Boundless, Unlimited, Ceaseless, Continuous.*

057 – SNOW SEARCH

Miss Smilla's Feeling for Snow. The letters are all displaced by one place in the alphabet.

058 – MADONNA MUDDLE

Desperately Seeking Susan. Take the middle letter of each word.

059 – MEAL MUDDLE

Brakfast at Tiffany's. Take the first and last letters of alternate words.

060 – MEAN-MINDED

Take the initial letter of each word and then write down the previous letter to it in alphabetical order. Continue like this until you have done the same thing with all the words and you will find that you have: *Anger, Rages, Shout, Stamp, Thump, Fists.*

061 – MORSE MUDDLE

A rose by any other name would smell as sweet. I turned all the letters into Morse but then swapped them in pairs so, for example, AR OS EB YA NY became RA SO BE AY YN.

Answers Answers Answ

062 – INCOGNITO

The name is *Brian White*. The letters are represented by their mirror positions in the alphabet e.g. B – second from the beginning, becomes Y second from the end. R ninth from the end, becomes I – ninthfrom the beginning. Answers: 1. *Y*, 2. *I*, 3. *R* (*Robert Redford*), 4. *Z*, 5. *M*, 6. *D*, 7. *S* (*Star*), 8. *R* (*Romulus and Remus*), 9. *G* (*Garibaldi*), 10. *V.*

063 – 6 OF THE BEST: WRITERS

These are all done by alphabetic displacement.

Hemingway, Roth, Salinger, Hawthorne, Melville, Whitman

I	N	F	M	W	W	J	M	M	M	F
F						M				
N						F				
J	U	R	W	K	B	Q				I
O						Y	D			K
H						M	P			R
X						T	W			M
B						W	L			P
Z						S	K			E
						J	Z			W

064 – MORSE MUDDLE

Silent pond, frog jumps. Splash! This is one of the most famous haiku by Basho. The whole thing is a grid code with the grid references given in Morse.

	•–	–•••	–•–•	–••	•
•–	A	B	C	D	E
–•••	F	G	H	IJ	K
–•–•	L	M	N	O	P
–••	Q	R	S	T	U
•	V	W	X	Y	Z

065 – MOUNTAIN HIGH

Simply take the final letter of each word. *Everest, Rushmore, Fuji, Etna.*

066 – NAMING NAMES

Lisa, Anne, Nick and Neil. The letters are displaced just one place in the alphabet. The one letter of each name is placed in each set of squares. The letters are always in the same place in each grid e.g. the letters for LISA are always top left.

067 – INCOGNITO

The name is *Susan Black*. Each letter is displaced three places in the alphabet e.g. S becomes V. The answers to the questions are: 1. *V*, 2. *X*, 3. *Vivaldi*, 4. *D-day*, 5. *Q*, 6. *East*, 7. *Oklahoma*, 8. *Dungeon*, 9. *Frugal*, 10. *Native American*.

068 – PERPLEXING PROBLEM

It was the night before Christmas. A pangram is a sentence that uses all the letters of the alphabet. The one I used was "J.Q. Schwartz flung D.V. Pike my box." You may think this a little obscure but it is a famous pangram and is frequently used.

J	Q	S	C	H	W
A	*B*	*C*	*D*	*E*	*F*
A	R	T	Z	F	L
G	*H*	*I*	*J*	*K*	*L*
U	N	G	D	V	P
M	*N*	*O*	*P*	*Q*	*R*
I	K	E	M	Y	B
S	*T*	*U*	*V*	*W*	*X*
O	X				
Y	*Z*				